MINISTERO DELLA PUBBLICA ISTRUZIONE
DIREZIONE GENERALE DELLE ANTICHITÀ E BELLE ARTI

GUIDE-BOOKS TO THE MUSEUMS, GALLERIES AND MONUMENTS OF ITALY

PAOLA DELLA PERGOLA

THE BORGHESE GALLERY IN ROME

(115 ILLUSTRATIONS)

(Trans. by M. E. STANLEY)

THIRTEENTH EDITION

ISTITUTO POLIGRAFICO DELLO STATO
LIBRERIA DELLO STATO

No. 43

OF THE SERIES OF

GUIDE-BOOKS TO THE MUSEUMS, GALLERIES AND MONUMENTS OF ITALY

*

Stampato in Italia - Printed in Italy

(8251049) ISTITUTO POLIGRAFICO DELLO STATO - ROMA - MCMLXIX

HISTORICAL ACCOUNT

*T*HE BORGHESE GALLERY *came into existence, at the beginning of the seventeenth century, as the result of the artistic tastes and interests of both Prince Camillo, who was raised to the See of Peter in 1605 under the name of Paul V, and his nephew Scipione Caffarelli Borghese, who became cardinal at the age of thirty, and whom the provident pope loaded with honours.*

The Borghese Palace in Campus Martius already contained important works of art, but when Scipione Borghese commissioned the Dutch architect Jan Van Santen (known as Vasanzio in Italy) to erect a richly ornamented suburban villa in the middle of a vineyard belonging to his family, it was not so much his intention to create a place of abode or a pleasure resort, as to provide a natural setting for the treasures of art which Paul V's patronages and the diligent zeal of his dependents enabled him to gather from all parts of Italy. Three years were needed, from 1613 to 1616, to build the villa. At the same time the vineyards were turned into picturesque or romantic gardens and parks, with lakes and woody recesses opening out into wide sunlit clearings; and herms, statues and sarcophagi lined all the avenues.

When, in a poem written in 1613, Scipione Francucci commemorated the splendour of the Borghese collection, it could already boast of being the principal nucleus of paintings and sculpture which in later years created the fame of the Gallery. In 1650 Jacopo Manilli gave a detailed description of it, including the decoration (" La Villa Borghese fuori di Porta Pinciana ,,), but nothing remains today of the ornamentation done during Scipione Borghese's time, with the exception of four little rooms on the top floor where the dragon and the eagle are coupled for the first time in the decoration of the painted wooden ceilings.

As it stands today, with its many frescoes and ornamentations, statues and bas-reliefs over the doors, on the fireplaces, and in the decoration of every room, the villa goes back to the middle of the eighteenth century, when Marcantonio Borghese, fired with enthusiasm equal to that of Cardinal Scipione, summoned the architect Antonio Asprucci, and the painter Mariano Rossi, together with a large troup of decorators (amongst which were Pacetti, Righi, Laboureur, Unterbergher, Gagnereaux, Giuseppe Cades, Conca, etc.) to complete the cardinal's original project. The arrangement of the so—called Hall of the Emperors, with its many marbles of every colour and kind and its harmonious, restrained magnificence, belongs to this period and to Asprucci. This adjustment of the Villa, which however only contained the sculpture, since the pictures were still at Palazzo Borghese, was described by Ennio Quirino Visconti (" Sculture del Palazzo della Villa Borghese a Porta Pinciana ,, , 1796), and by Antonio Nibby (" Monumenti scelti della Villa Borghese ,, , 1832).

The collection suffered considerably between 1802 and 1809 when Prince Camillo, the husband of Pauline Bonaparte, started to break it up by selling several of the pictures in Paris (the Supper of Emmaus by Caravaggio, and St. Catherine by Raphael being among them), and when, in exchange for the fief of Leucadio in Piemonte, he gave France over two hundred pieces of classical sculpture, amongst which were the Mars, the Gladiator, the Hermaphrodites, the Altar of the Twelve Gods, the Wild Boar, and other important works of art which are still exhibited, under the Borghese name, at the Louvre.

During the first half of the nineteenth century, another promoter of art appeared in this princely family, who again built up the impoverished collection. This was Francesco Borghese who increased the classical part in particular, and created the Museum, which was to have been called the Sabine Museum. Excavations carried out near Tusculum, on his family estate, brought to light the five large mosaics with fighting gladiators and hunting scenes, which decorate the pavement of the entrance hall; and the architect Luigi Canina, who planned the approach from Porta del Popolo, arranged the works of art in the Villa. However, all the pictures were still housed in the Palace in Campus Martius.

Finally in 1891 the two parts were brought together in the Villa, and in 1902 the whole collection, which had been in the hands of Trustees, became the property of the State.

In 1893 Adolfo Venturi compiled the Catalogue of the Borghese Gallery, on the basis of Giovanni Piancastelli's manuscript notes, giving a first attempt at descriptive criticism. Still of fundamental value are the contributions of Roberto Longhi, published in " Precisioni nelle Gallerie Italiane: La Galleria Borghese ,, , Rome 1928. From that time onwards critics have given the collection a place of world—wide importance. This admirable artistic assemblage, which has been considerably enlarged by the addition of gifts and acquisitions (such as Tobias and the Angel by Savoldo, the Courtesan by Ter Brugghen, two busts of Scipione Borghese by Bernini, and a model by the same sculptor for the equestrian monument of Louis XIV of France) bears witness, in every detail, of the aesthetic taste of one of the most liberal and enlightened phases of Italian culture.

4

THE BORGHESE GALLERY IN ROME

GROUND FLOOR

THE VESTIBULE

Examples of Roman sculpture, of no great artistic value, are gathered in the vestibule of the Museum. The following are worthy of note:

XXV. This number refers to three fragments of a bas-relief formerly thought to have belonged to the triumphal arch erected in honour of Claudius. Later research has however shown that they were part of a *triumphal frieze* of the Emperor Trajan, better preserved elements of which are inserted in the decoration of the Arch of Constantine (M. Pallottino).

XIII, XVIII. Two large porphyry columns on either side of the portal.

VI. Bas-relief representing the *nine Muses*.

CCXXXXI. Group representing *Bacchus with a little girl* who is perhaps deceased. The iconography of this group is rather rare. Restored in several places.

CXXII. Statue of *Hercules*. Only the torso is antique; the restorations belong to the time of the Renaissance.

CLXVIII. Statue of *Diana* (?). The torso is antique; the head, which has been added, is the work of the Renaissance.

CLXX. Statue of a *Nymph* holding a shell. Probably part of the decoration of a fountain.

CCXXXV. Statue of *Pan*. Roman art.

XXX. A large marble *candelabrum* with a conventional decoration of ivy leaves.

I. Another large *candelabrum* decorated with Bacchic masks.

THE ENTRANCE HALL

This great entrance hall of the Museum is of true Roman magnificence. It is remarkable for its vastness, its rich decoration, and its monumental statuary. The ceiling was frescoed in 1774 by MARIANO ROSSI from Sciacca (Sicily, 1731–1807) and represents the Story of *Marcus Furius Camillus* who is seen breaking the negotiations with Brennus. The ornamentation consists of a well balanced combination of painting, sculpture and architecture, carried out by various artists: VINCENZO PACETTI (1746–1820), FRANCESCO CARRADORI (1747–1825), MASSIMILIANO LABOUREUR (1739–1812), GIOVANNI MONTI (flourished around 1780), TOMMASO RIGHI (1727–1802); whereas the grotesques were done by PIETRO ROTATI (active somewhere about 1780), and the animal decorations, of which the one showing a *hen with her chickens*, on the right wall, immediately became famous, by WENCESLAS PETER (1745–1829).

The large high relief of Roman period, on the wall facing the entrance, represents *Marcus Curtius leaping into the chasm*. Incorporated in the pavement are the five third–century A. D. mosaics found at Torrenuova, near Tusculum, during excavations carried out on the Borghese estate. They represent hunting scenes and fights between gladiators and wild animals.

The sculpture:

XXXV. A colossal, " serenely majestic ,, (Helbig) head of *Isis*, identified by the lotus flower on her forehead. Partially restored in the flower, the arched eyebrows, the nose, a portion of the neck and the tips of the hair.

XXXVI. A colossal *Satyr* from Palazzo Sacchetti in Via Giulia. In spite of the many restorations (the head, the two arms, the legs and the trunk of the tree), the movement is spontaneous and vivacious.

XXXVII. A colossal head of *Juno* or, according to Helbig, a Muse.

XXXVIII. Head of *Vespasian*, on a Portasanta bust.

XXXIX. Statue of an *Emperor*, perhaps Tiberius, although the head, which portrays him, was added during a restoration.

XL. Statue of *Meleager*, from a fourth–century original attributed to Skopas, with slight variations in the details. The head, the neck, part of the chest, the right arm and right leg are restorations.

XLI. Statue of *Augustus* as Pontifex Maximus.

VIL. Statue of a *Priestess*, belonging to the Antonine period. The base upon which it stands refers to Petronia Musa.

VL. A *dancing Satyr*. A colossal statue of which only the torso is antique.

IVL. Statue of a *man wearing a toga*, supposed to be Pompey (Bernoulli). The head is an addition. On the base is the representation of a *sacrifice to Minerva*.

IIIL. A male head of the first century, on an alabaster bust.

IIL. A colossal head of *Hadrian*.

XLIX. A colossal statue of *Bacchus*. The torso and part of the legs are certainly antique, and may possibly have originally belonged to a Satyr.

L. A colossal head of *Antoninus*, formerly at Palazzo Borghese in Campus Martius.

LI. A male head of an unknown person, in Parian marble on a Portasanta bust.

LII. Statue of *Diana*.

XXXIII. Statue of *Diana*, of the time of the Antonines. The head is a portrait of a Roman matron.

XXXIV. A male bust with a breastplate of black and grey marble, and an alabaster paludamentum.

Nos. XXXVI, XLII, and XLIX rest upon three fragments representing *Bacchic scenes*, which all belonged to the same monument; they are of exceptionally fine workmanship. Twelve eighteenth-century *busts of Emperors*, in white and grey-veined marble, placed in niches round the upper part of the walls, add a note of colour to the decorative scheme of the hall.

ROOM I

The painted decoration and the architectural perspectives on the vaulted ceiling and on the two shorter walls are by GIOVANNI BATTISTA MARCHETTI (Siena, 1730–1800). DOMENICO DE ANGELIS (Ponzano, still active in 1803) painted the *Judgement of Paris*, in the centre of the ceiling, as well as *Juno imploring Aeolus to destroy the Trojan ships, Aeneas escaping from burning Troy, the Fates spinning the destiny of Rome*, and *Venus interceding with Jupiter for Aeneas*, in the four surrounding pictures.

VINCENZO PACETTI (1746–1820) did the bas-reliefs over the doors. The four friezes on the upper part of the walls were sculptured by AGOSTINO PENNA (died in 1800).

The sculpture:

LXXIV. A seventeenth-century bas-relief representing a little *Cupid borne by an eagle*.

LXXII. *Venus* adorning herself, assisted by Cupid whose function is purely ornamental.

LXXV. This number refers to two bas-reliefs facing each other on opposite walls. They both originally formed part of a third century A.D. relief representing *Apollo and the nine Muses*.

CCLXXI. JEAN ANTOINE HOUDON (Versailles, 1741–1828), *St. John the Baptist*. The original plaster model, carried out between 1764 and 1768, while the artist was in Rome, for a statue of the Baptist which was to have paired with the one of St. Bruno in the Church of S. Maria degli Angeli. It keeps to a cold academic precision, revealing the influence of this neo-classic sculptor's study of archaeology.

7

LXXI. Bas–relief found at Torrenuova in the seventeenth century, supposed to represent the *upbringing of Telephus* (Winckelmann).

LXIX. A small statue which, like numbers LXV and CVIC, stood in the grounds of the Villa in the eighteenth century, and represents a *boy of the populace*, as testified by the simple cloak and the cap (pileus) worn by the lower classes. It is derived from a Hellenistic original, and its urchin charm and fine quality are apparent even in this Roman copy.

LXVIII. Statue of *Ceres*. The attribute of Flora has been added at some later period, and the head is modern. The altar on which it stands represents a sacrificial scene.

LXVII. A basalt *head of a man*, on a loricated bust, thought to be Septimius Severus.

LXVI. An idealized statue of a *matron*, whose head–dress is reminiscent of Julia the daughter of Titus. It was, for no particular reason, thought to be a symbolic representation of Hope.

LXV. A small statue of a boy, similar to No. LXIX.

LXIV. Bas–relief representing *Ajax raping Cassandra* Hellenistic Style.

LXII. *Leda and the Swan*, almost entirely done over again in the nineteenth century.

LXI. Bas–relief representing *Minos*, with his mother Europa, about to sacrifice to Poseidon. It formed the side of a sarcophagus, as seen from a drawing in the Collection of Prints in Berlin (Helbig).

CVIC. A small statue of a boy, similar to Nos. LXIX and LXV.

LVIII. Statue of *Venus*, a poor reproduction of a well known statue by the sculptor Kallimachos. It is much restored and has a modern head.

LVI. Statue of a *Muse*, on a pedestal with Bacchic representations.

CCLXXII. PIETRO BRACCI (Roma, 1700–1773), *Bust of Pope Clement XII Corsini*. There is a studied attempt at psychological expression in the face, and an accentuated decorativism in the draperies. Bracci is however one of the best representative of eighteenth–century sculpture in Rome.

LV. Statue of a youth, in Lunensis marble.

In the niches round the upper part of the walls are seven busts of a decorative nature. In the centre of the room:

LIV. ANTONIO CANOVA (Possagno, 1757–1822), *Pauline Borghese Bonaparte as Venus Victrix*. The artist has found a facile means of expression for his talent in the natural, nimble grace of the lady. They both take part in this statue which Canova executed in Rome in 1805, according to the classical canons of art, but which is softened by the alluring beauty of his young model who seems to take the sculptor by the hand, and vanquish the cold rigidity of the rules. Nowhere else has Canova succeeded in portraying such a tender effigy and such a relaxed body, or so ably caught the lady's prankish moods. In this piece of sculpture, which is certainly his masterpiece, he dominates the material, and everything becomes unusually tractable and light. Though from the front the couch and the figure may not seem to be in proper proportion, the successful combination of the drapery and the nude, seen from behind, makes up for this defect.

Room II

The picture in the centre of the ceiling represents the *Fall of Phaeton*, and was painted by FRANCESCO CACCIANIGA (Milan, 1700–1781). The ornamentations are by LUIGI AGRICOLA (1751–1790), and the reliefs on the pilasters by TOMMASO RIGHI (Rome, 1727–1802).

The sculpture:

LXXVIII. *Herm of Pan.*

LXXXI. A relief representing the *Birth of Venus.*

LXXX. A frieze recounting four episodes connected with the *arrival of the Amazons at Troy, while Hector's family is bewailing death*:

1) Andromache with the infant Astyanax on her knees; two weeping women by her, and an old woman, perhaps Hecuba, approaching with a message.

2) Penthesiles, Queen of the Amazons, being received by Priam. She is leading her horse and followed by a companion. Behind Priam are four Trojans and a youth who has been identified as Paris.

3) Hecuba clasps the urn containing Hector's ashes, while Polydorus comes to comfort her.

4) The Amazons prepare for battle.

At either end of the frieze, which was meant to crown a sarcophagus (not the one on which it rests today) are tragic masks of the Hellenic period belonging to some other monument.

LXXIX. The front of a sarcophagus with a representation of the *Labours of Hercules*, belonging to the time of the Antonines. In high relief, beneath the five arches of a Corinthian portico, are the episodes of his contests with the Nemean lion, the Lernean hydra, the Erymanthian boar, the brazen-footed Arcadian stag, and the Stymphalian birds, one of which lies dead at his feet.

No. VC, opposite, in this same room, is the other side of the sarcophagus, giving five more episodes: his contests with the

Cretian bull, Geryones, Hippolyte Queen of the Amazons, the Dragon that guarded the Gardens of the Hesperides, and the Centaur Nessus.

Both have fine plinths with hunting scenes in bas-relief.

LXXXII. Herm of *Bacchus*. Only the upper part is antique.

LXXXIII. Head of Hercules, of the Farnese Hercules type. The cippus on which it is placed is dedicated to Julius Eutychianus.

LXXXIV. The *infant Hercules* with the skin of the Nemean lion over his shoulder.

LXXXV. Bust of *Sappho* on a cippus dedicated to Flavia Variana. The prototype of this portrait dates back to the fifth century.

LXXXVI. *Herm of Hercules* with the skin of the Nemean lion.

LXXXVII. Front of a sarcophagus with figures of Nereids and Tritons.

LXXXVIII. Fragment of a frieze with a conventional floral motive.

LXXXIX. Bas-relief representing Jupiter, Juno, Minerva, the Dioscuri, and the Sun rising in his quadriga, while Night retires. Of second-century Roman workmanship.

XC. Another *Herm of Hercules* wrapped in the skin of the Nemean lion.

IXC. Bust of a woman, with the attributes of Isis added at a later date. The cippus is dedicated to Claudius Felix.

VIIIC. The *infant Bacchus*.

VIIC. *Bust of a youth*, perhaps Alexander.

VIC. *Herm of Bacchus*, of archaicizing type.

VC. The other part of sarcophagus No. LXXIX.

IVC. Bas-relief representing the *Birth of Apollo and Artemis*.

IIIC. Bas-relief with a *Bacchanalian* representation.

IIC. Another *Herm of Bacchus*, of archaicizing type.

IC. A small statue of *Bacchus resting his hand on an amphora*. In the restoration he has been given the head of a Faun.

C. *Venus*, a copy of the so-called Capitoline Venus. The cippus which acts as a base is dedicated to T. Aurelius Trypho.

CXXXII. A very rare *green porphyry amphora*, resting on a quadrangular base of red and green porphyry, executed in 1787 by ANTOINE GUILLOME GRANDJACQUET (Reugney, 1731–1801).

CII. Statue of *Apollo*. It stands on a cippus dedicated to Marcus Ulpius Heliadius.

CIII. The *infant Hercules* in the attitude of the Farnese Hercules.

LXXVII. GIAN LORENZO BERNINI (Naples, 1598–1680), *David*. An early work by Bernini, who carried it out in 1619, and portrayed himself in the strained features of the intrepid youth. The vibrant sense of movement by which the sculptor breaks away from the models of the Renaissance, gives the figure an incentive which is new in art, and marks the triumphant affirmation of the Baroque. The intersecting surfaces, the crossing diagonals, the tension of the body in a space which also forms part of the sculpture as a whole, help to give an impression of extraordinarily intense action, which is preluded in the contractions of the face, in the iron will emphasized by the sealed lips. The figure is not portrayed photografically. It is itself both prelude and consequence, and comes to life independently.

The paintings:

23. ANNIBALE CARRACCI (Bologna, 1560–1609), *Samson in Prison* (canvas: 1,95 × 1,35). Though formerly attributed to Titian, this picture is today unanimously held to be one of the academic paintings done by Annibale Carracci during his stay in Rome.

6. NICOLÒ DELL'ABATE (Modena, 1509–1571), *Landscape with a Stag Hunt* (canvas: 1,16 × 1,59).

180. GUIDO RENI (Bologna, 1575–1642), *Moses with the Tables of the Law* (canvas: 1,85 × 1,30). This painting, which belongs to a period when Reni was influenced by Caravaggio's effects of light, is mentioned by Malvasia, and comes from Palazzo Barberini by Monte di Pietà. It is a fine picture, carried out with great ability and with a profound sense of colour.

8. GIROLAMO DA CARPI (Ferrara, 1501–1556), *Landscape with a Procession of Magicians* (canvas: 1,16 × 1,59). This, like No. 6, was also attributed to Nicolò dell'Abate, but the difference in the hand is obvious. Gamba is responsible for the attribution to Girolamo da Carpi, which seems to be feasible.

192. PIER FRANCESCO MOLA (Coldraro, 1612–1666), *The Liberation of St. Peter* (canvas: 1,91 × 1,35) was already mentioned in the inventaries of the Borghese Gallery at the end of the eighteenth century. The action is imposing, though somewhat rhetorical.

In the niches over the doors are five busts, of late Roman period which perform a purely decorative function.

ROOM III

GIOVAN BATTISTA MARCHETTI carried out the decoration of the ceiling, and PIETRO ANGELETTI (Rome, 1758–1786) painted the *Metamorphosis of Daphne* in the centre, as it were, accompanying Bernini's group which was to be placed in this hall.

The sculpture:

CXXIII. A small much restored statue, perhaps of an Amazon. Only the torso is antique.

CXXI. Statuette of *Apollo*.

CXX. A *colossal head*, thought to be of Lucilla (Nibby). It has however been erroneously placed on a female bust. It represents a type of ephebus, and can be dated to the second-third century.

CXIX. Two *alabaster vases*, on red granite columns, belonging to the seventeenth century.

CXXXXII. An *alabaster lion*, belonging to the late Roman period, which evidently formed part of the decoration of a fountain.

CXVII. Statue of *Apollo* of archaic type.

CXVI. A marble *amphora* with the representation of a Bacchic dance. It rests on a triangular base with the figures of Venus, Bacchus and Mercury.

CVII. A decorative group for a fountain or garden. A charming scene with peasants and fishermen, in Hellenistic style. It has been repeatedly restored and whole portions of it have been entirely re-made.

CXI. A small *female statue* to which the attributes of Isis have been added.

CX. A *boy playing with two ducks*. Nibby considers it to belong to the time of the Antonines. This too is a motive taken from Hellenistic art which often represented scenes of this kind.

CIX. Two *pavonazzetto vases* on columns of the same marble, belonging to the seventeenth century.

CVIII. A small statue of *Venus*, of the Capitoline type.

CVI. A *boy playing with a duck*. Much restored. This statue, which belongs to the Roman period, also repeats a Hellenistic type.

CV. GIAN LORENZO BERNINI (Naples, 1598-1680), *Apollo and Daphne*. Sculptured in 1624. Here the realization of motion, which particularly marks the early Baroque, is expressed in lyrical terms The sculptor has portrayed the moment when the pursuing Apollo is about to grasp Daphne who is turned to laurel. However, not only this particular instant has been caught by the marble; behind the representation is the whole series of motives that precede it, and before it all those still to come. The pliant marble vies with painting in softening the shadows and in achieving supple transitions. Never had sculpture attained such sureness and ability, or such delicacy, as in the figure of the Nymph, round whose body the bark already clings. On the base, the eagle and the dragon (the two motives in the Borghese armorial bearings) each hold a notice, one with Ovid's distichs, and the other with the lines composed by Maffeo Barberini, giving the legend a Christian meaning.

" Mollia cinguntur tenui praecordia libro — in frondem crines in ramos brachia crescunt — pes modo tam velox pigris radicibus haeret ,,.

" Quisquis amans sequitur fugitivae gaudia formae — Fronde manus implet baccas sed carpit amaras ,,.

On the walls are two large paintings:

14. LUDOVICO CIGOLI (Ludovico Cardi, Empoli, 1559–1613), *Joseph and the Wife of Potiphar* (canvas: 2,25 × 1,50) dated: 1610.

15. GIOVANNI BAGLIONE (Rome, 1571–1644), *Judith and Holofernes* (canvas: 2,20 × 1,50). In this picture, Caravaggio's fiercest compeditor has succumbed to the influence of his forceful rival.

Over the doors:

12. PAUL BRILL (Antwerp, 1554–1626), *Landscape* (canvas: 0,84 × 1,12).

13. PAUL BRILL (Antwerp, 1554–1626), *Landscape* (canvas: 0,78 × 1,06).

THE CHAPEL

This room, which was brought to light in 1930 by Achille Bertini Calosso, is frescoed by CLAUDE DERUET (Nancy-Lorraine, 1588–1660) who painted the *Assumption* in it, as well as the figures of *St. Charles Borromeo* and *St. Frances of Rome* on either side, between ornamental decorations and medallons. Overhead, the *Eternal Father*. On the opposite wall: No. 16, GIOVANNI LANFRANCO (Parma, 1582–1648), a large canvas representing *Norandino and Lucilla Surprised by the Ogre* (canvas: 2,60 × 3,88) taken from Ariosto's *Orlando Furioso*, Canto XVII. The picture was painted for the Borghese Villa at Frascati.

CXII. *Female bust* of the late Roman period.

LXXIII. Another *female figure*, thought to represent Medicine, though for no particular reason.

478. MATTHIAE WALLBAUM (Kiel, 1554–1632), *Little altar*. Silver and palisandes.

ROOM IV

This is known as the Hall of the Emperors, owing to the eighteen seventeenth-century busts in porphyry and alabaster placed round the walls. The ornamentation of the ceiling is by GIOVAN BATTISTA MARCHETTI, and DOMENICO DE ANGELIS painted the three canvases with the *story of Galatea*. CESARE AGNATTI, PETER RUDIEZ, AGOSTINO PENNA, VINCENZO PACETTI, TOMMASO RIGHI, FRANCESCO CARRADORI, MAXIMILIAN LABOUREUR, and LUIGI SALIMENI (the same artists who decorated the great entrance hall at the time of Marcantonio Borghese) did the bas–reliefs in marble and stucco, and the mosaics on the walls.

The sumptuous polichrome effect created by the many kinds of marbles that abound everywhere, from the pavement and walls, to the tables, columns, amphoras and basins gathered in the hall, make this one of the most precious examples of the aesthetic taste of the eighteenth century.

CXXXV. A seventeenth–century bust of *Scipio Africanus*.

CXXV. A red porphyry *crater* (seventeenth century).

CXXVI. Statue of a *young woman* holding a mask in her left hand, which however is a restoration.

CXXXVI. Bust of *Agrippa* (seventeenth century).

CXXXXVIII. Bust of *Cicero* (seventeenth century).

CXXIX. Statue of *Diana*.

CXXX. SILVIO DA VELLETRI (seventeenth century). Vase of antique black marble, on a porphyry table with an amethist base.

CXXXI. Two oriental alabaster columns with gilt metal capitals and marble pedestals with alabaster inlay (seventeenth century).

CLXV. A large *sepulchral urn* of red porphyry from the Mausoleum of Hadrian. Roman period.

CXXXIII. SILVIO DA VELLETRI (seventeenth century). Vase of antique black marble on a porphyry and amethist table, similar to No. CXXX.

CXXXIX. A seventeenth–century bust of *Augustus*.

CLXII. A seventeenth–century bust of *Tiberius*.

CXXXVII. Statue of *Artemis*.

CXXXVIII. A red porphyry *crater*, like No. CXXV.

CLVII. Bust of *Caligula*, of seventeenth-century workmanship.

CXXXXIII. Statue of *Bacchus*. Only the torso is antique.

CCXLIX. ANTONIO SUSINI (Florence, died in 1624), *The Torture of Dirce* (bronze). Signed and dated: Ant. Susini Fior. Opus A. D. MDCXIII. This is one of the copies (Susini made several) of the famous group known as the Farnese Bull, now at the National Museum of Naples, found in 1546 in the Baths of Caracalla in Rome. According to Pliny, the original, which belongs to Hellenistic art, was by Apollonios and Tauriskos, two artists from Tralles.

CXXXXI. A red porphyry table with rests formed of winged lions in Moricone alabaster. Of seventeenth–century workmanship.

CXXXXIX. A seventeenth-century bust of *Nero*.

CXXXXV. Herm of *Bacchus*, with a bronze head in archaic style on a red oriental alabaster stand. This too belongs to the seventeenth century, although Nibby takes it for antique.

CXXVII. Bust of *Galba*, belonging to the seventeenth century.

CXXXXVII. MAXIMILIAN LABOUREUR (Rome, 1739–1812). Vase of Lunense marble, with a representation of *Spring*.

CLII. A seventeenth-century bust of *Otto*.

CXXXX. A seventeenth-century bust of *Vitellius*.

CL. MAXIMILIAN LABOUREUR (cf. No. CXXXXVII). Vase of Lunense marble representing *Summer*.

CLVIII. Another seventeenth-century bust of *Vitellius*.

CLI. Bust of *Vespasian*.

CLIII. MAXIMILIAN LABOUREUR (cf. Nos. CL and CXXXXVII). Vase of Lunense marble with a representation of *Autumn*.

CLV. Another seventeenth-century bust of *Vespasian*.

CXXXXIV. A seventeenth-century bust of *Titus*.

CLVI. MAXIMILIAN LABOUREUR (cf. No. CL, etc.). Vase of Lunense marble with a representation of *Winter*.

CLIV. Bust of *Trajan*. Seventeenth century.

CLXI. Statue of a *Nymph with a dolphin*. A copy of a Hellenistic original. It was perhaps used to decorate a fountain.

CLIX. A red porphyry table supported by winged lions of Moricone alabaster, similar to No. CXXXXI.

7386. GIAN LORENZO BERNINI (Naples, 1598–1680), *Neptune*. A bronze model, carried out somewhere around 1622, from the National Gallery of Antique Art. According to Muñoz this is a variation of the statuary group of Neptune and Glaucus made for Cardinal Montalto's villa. The original group has recently been bought by the Albert and Victoria Museum, London.

CXXXXVI. A porphyry head of *Juno* on an alabaster bust. This, like the busts of the Emperors, belongs to the seventeenth century, although Nibby takes it for antique.

In the centre of the hall:

CLXIII. A small seventeenth-century urn of antique black marble, supported by four winged dragons (the Borghese emblem). It stands on a red porphyry table supported by white marble sphinxes. This too belongs to the seventeenth century.

CLXIV. A large red porphyry *cup* (seventeenth century).

CLXVI. Another large cup like the aforegoing.

CLXVII. A small urn of antique black marble supported by winged dragons, on a red porphyry table with white marble sphinxes, pairing with No. CLXIII.

15

CCLXVIII. GIAN LORENZO BERNINI (Naples, 1598–1680), *The Rape of Proserpina.* This statue is usually thought to be the result of a collaboration between Bernini and his father Pietro, owing to the fact that the composition is conceived in a more traditional and academic manner, and because of a coldness of form which separates it from the two aforegoing statues, especially in the figure of Pluto.

The group is supposed to have been executed before the David and the Apollo and Daphne. It represents the myth of Proserpina who was carried off by the King of Hades; the three-headed dog (Cerberus) is the symbol of the nether world to which the maiden is about to be taken. In spite of the obvious mannerism of the whole, the softness of the flesh and the pathetic expression in the figure of Proserpina preannounces the pictorial trend of Gian Lorenzo's later creations.

ROOM V

The ceiling, painted by GIOVAN BATTISTA MARCHETTI and NICOLA BUONVICINI (active at the end of the seventeenth century) represents incidents in the myth of Hermaphroditus and Salmacis. VINCENZO PACETTI did the little figures of Cupids that support the cornice.

The sculpture:

CCXXXX. Statue of a *Roman matron* of the third century A. D.

CLXIX. A female statue of the time of the Antonines. The symbolic ears of corn, turning the statue into a figure of Ceres, are the additions of a late restoration.

CCXXXXII. A female statue of the time of the Antonines.

CLXXI. Bust of the *Emperor Titus.*

CLXXII. *Sleeping Hermaphroditus.* A late copy, and not one of the best, of the famous Hellenistic type. A much finer copy, which once belonged to the Borghese collection, was sold by Prince Camillo to France, and is now at the Louvre. This one was restored by ANDREA BERGONDI (Rome, active around 1767) who completely remade the mattress, the whole of the head as far as the neck, the right elbow, the left leg, and other secondary details.

CLXXIII. An oriental alabaster amphora on a red porphyry base (seventeenth century).

CLXXIV. Bust of a *young woman,* supposed to be Sappho, in accordance with a well known type, the original of which belongs to Greek art of the fifth century.

CCXXVIII. Statue of a *Satyr*, derived from a Praxitelian type.

CCXXVI. Another statue of a *Satyr*, similar to the preceding one.

VIII. Fragment of a small, finely worked copy of the Athena Parthenos by Phidias. Roman period.

CLXXX. A fragment of a statue representing Ganymedes, according to Nibby. Remarkable for the purity of the Greek marble. It was brought to light in 1835 during excavations in Via Nomentana.

CLXXXI. An archaic female portrait–head (sixth century B. C.) on a Roman bust.

Over the doors:

18. PAUL BRIL (Antwerp, 1554–1626), *Landscape* (canvas: 0,66 × 0,90).

19. PAUL BRIL (Antwerp, 1554–1626), *Landscape* (canvas: 0,66 × 0,90).

21. PAUL BRIL (Antwerp, 1554–1626), *Landscape* (canvas: 0,66 × 0,90).

20. PAUL BRIL (Antwerp, 1554–1626), *Landscape* (canvas: 0,66 × 0,90).

The Roman mosaic with two fishermen in a boat, in the pavement, and the other similar one beneath the window, belong to a late period and are of rough workmanship.

ROOM VI

The ornamental motives of the ceiling in this room are also by GIOVANNI BATTISTA MARCHETTI. The *Banquet of the Gods* in the centre is the work of LAURENCE PECHEUX (Lyons 1740–1820), and the stucco bas–reliefs with Corybantic dances placed round the walls were carried out by VINCENZO PACETTI (Castelbolognese, 1746–1820).

The large portrait–relief in red porphyry, over the door on the garden side, represents Pope Paul V (Camillo Borghese), the uncle and patron of Cardinal Scipione; and the large antique cameo, over the door leading into room VII, to which the bust and helmet were added in the sixteenth century to turn it into a portrait of Alexander, represented one of the Dioscuri, according to Nibby.

The sculpture:

CIC. This statue of *Aesculapius with his son Telesphorus* provides an example of Attic sculpture.

CIVC. Sarcophagus, with the figure of the deceased lying on the lid. On either side, Nereids, Tritons and sea monsters

CIIIC. A female statue belonging to the Antonine period. Perhaps an Empress.

CIIC. A high relief with *figures wearing togas*, belong to the Severian period.

CVC. Statue of a *girl*, belonging to the Antonine period.

Lent by the Bernini Heirs:

GIAN LORENZO BERNINI (Naples, 1598–1680), *Truth*. This large female figure, begun in 1645 when the sculptor fell out of favour, after the death of Urban VIII, and was sent away from the pontifical court, was to have represented Truth revealed by Time. The second statue was however never carried out, and the controversy, rarely in accordance with art, is expressed in a worn out rhetorical piece of work, where the splendid concurrence of form and pictoricalism experimented by Bernini loses itself in a heavy pleonastic naturalism.

CVIIC. *Leda*, a poor copy of a Hellenistic original.

CXV. Statuette of a boy, in Hellenistic style.

CLXXXIV. A marble high relief on a touchstone background, with a frame of antique yellow marble, formerly assigned to Algardi. It representes *three sleeping babies*, carried out in imitation of a favourite motive in Hellenistic art, from which its inspiration is derived. It is however of seventeenth–century workmanship. The red granite table on which it is placed is supported by alabaster dolphins, and also belongs to the seventeenth century.

CXIII. *Cupid bound and weeping*, a Roman copy of a Hellenistic original.

CIXC. Statue of a *Nymph* obviously derived from the Vatican Danaid. The head, which is different in this case, was added during a restoration.

CXC. Group of *three female figures*, which, according to Helbig, has been so completely remodelled that it can no longer be considered antique. It represents the Three Ages, or the Three Fates.

CLXXXVII. Lid of a sarcophagus with a reclining female figure. Antonine period.

CLXXXVIII. Group of three figures in high relief, probably belonging to the first century.

CLXXXVI. Colossal head of Juno or Cybele. Second century Roman art.

CLXXXV. A figure wearing a toga.

508. FRANÇOIS DUQUESNOY (Brussels, 1594–1646). A touchstone bas–relief on a lapis lazuli ground representing a *Bacchanalia*. The two statues of Negro hunters on either side, one leading a lion (479), and the other a tiger (480), also of

touchstone, are by the same sculptor. They stand on a seventeenth-century table similar to the one opposite, in red granite supported by alabaster dolphins.

CLXXXIII. Statue of *Athena Parthenos,* a Roman copy of slight importance of a chryselephantine figure by Phidias.

In the centre of the room:

CLXXXII. PIETRO BERNINI (Sesto Fiorentino, 1563–1629), *Aeneas and Anchises.* This group, which was formerly attributed to Gian Lorenzo, can be certainly included among the smaller sized works of the father, Pietro. It represents Aeneas fleeing from the fire of Troy, carrying his father Anchises on his shoulders, and followed by his son Ascanius. Anchises is bearing the images of the Penates. Neither the separate figures nor the group as a whole possesses the suppleness or the freedom of action proper to Gian Lorenzo Bernini.

The paintings:

22. DOSSO DOSSI (Giovanni Luteri. Ferrara, 1470–1542) *Sts. Cosmas and Damian* (canvas: 2,25 × 1,57). Painted for the Hospital of S. Anna at Ferrara, and added to Scipione Borghese's collection in 1607.

347. BENVENUTO TISI called il GAROFALO (Ferrara, 1481–1559), *The Conversion of St. Paul* (canvas: 2,47 × 1,57). Dated MDXXXXV.

Over the doors:

405. GIOVAN MARIA MORANDI (Siena, 1622–1717), *The Transit of the Blessed Virgin.* A sketch, though complete and pictorically finished, for Morandi's large picture in the church of S. Maria della Pace, in Rome.

52. ANONYMUS (seventeenth century), *Cupid and Psyche* (canvas: 1,25 × 1,50).

ROOM VII

All the decoration of this room is carried out in Egyptian style, from the ornamentation of the ceiling by GIOVAN BATTISTA MARCHETTI, to the episodes of *Cybele offering her gifts to the Nile; the winged Anubis; Egyptian rites,* and the *story of Cleopatra* painted by TOMMASO CONCA (Gaeta, 1749 ca.–1816), the lotus flowers and palmettes, and the black marbles and the sphinxes over the doors.

The sculpture:

CCXXIV. An oriental alabaster amphora. The work of the seventeenth century.

CCXIX. A pharmacy amphora of antique black marble. Middle of the seventeenth century.

CCXXII. An oriental alabaster vase. Seventeenth century.

CXXII. A cup of antique red marble with knotted handles; the inside is sculptured with a design of broad leaves, fastened by a head of Medusa. It stands on a stem–shaped base of the same marble. Seventeenth century.

CCXX. An oriental alabaster vase, similar to CCXXII.

CCXXI. Amphora of antique black marble pairing with CCXIX.

CCXVIII. An oriental alabaster amphora, similar to CCXXIV.

CCXVII. Statue of *Athena*.

CCXVI. Statue of a *young girl*. Helbig considers it to be an original work of the Peloponnesian school, before Polycletus. The head, which is antique but much restored, would seem to belong to some other statue.

CCXV. Statue of *Venus Anadiomenes*.

CCIV. An oval basin of dark grey oriental granite, on a column of the same stone.

CCXIII. An alabaster amphora, similar to CCXXIV and CCXVIII.

CCXII. Head of *Ceres*, corwned with ears of corn, placed on an African bust.

XXXI. A Basalt *sphinx*, executed from CANINA's design, in imitation of CCVII.

CCXX. Basin of breccia corallina.

CCIX. A Roman statue of *Isis* figuring as Ceres, belonging to the time of Hadrian.

CCVIII. Basin of oriental granitello.

CCVII. A basalt *sphinx*. This one is antique.

CCV. An oriental alabaster amphora, similar to CCXXIV, CCXIII, and CCXVIII.

CCXIV. An oval basin of rare black and rose–white granite, on a column of the same rare stone, pairing with CCIV.

CCIII. Statue of *Paris*, derived from an original of which there is a better copy in the Vatican.

CCII. Statue of a *Priestess*, of Roman period, first century. The metal attributes are perhaps additions of the same period.

CCI. Statue of a dancing *Bacchante*.

CC. Statue of a *youth astride a dolphin*. The satyr's head is a later addition. It belongs to the Antonine period, and was probably a motive for a fountain. Some see a connection between it and the statue of Jonah in the Chigi chapel at S. Maria del Popolo.

In the pavement are three Roman mosaics with masks, two of which are male and the other female. Under the window is a fourth, with a representation of the Federal Pact observed by the ancient Italic people.

The three Empire chairs, in the window embrasure, are supposed to have been part of the furniture of Pauline Bonaparte Borghese's apartment.

Room VIII

The *Sacrifice of Silenus* on the ceiling, and the scenes of Satyrs, between ornamental motives by GIOVAN BATTISTA MARCHETTI, were painted by TOMMASO CONCA (Gaeta, 1749 ca.– 1815). In the centre of the room:

CCXXV. A *dancing Satyr.* Thorwaldsen added the forearms and clappers, but in an entirely arbitrary manner. The figure was probably playing the double tibia. The sense of sustained movement at the commencement of the dance, is particularly fine in this Roman copy of a bronze original of Lysippian sculpture.

The sculpture:

CLXXV. A Pentelic marble bust of *Tiberius.* Roman art of the first century.

CCXXXXIII. Bust of a *woman* of the Antonine period.

CCXXXXIV. Bust of a *woman* of the second–third century.

CCXXXI. Bust of *Minerva* wearing a helmet in the form of a head of Medusa. The work of the seventeenth century.

CCXXXVIII. Statue of a *Roman matron* of the IIIrd century. The mask was added during a later restoration, in order to make the figure represent a Muse.

CCXXXVII. Statue of *Thucydides,* or one of the Diadochi, idealized to resemble Jupiter. Here too the head has been added at some later date.

CCXXXVI. Statue of a *Roman matron,* belonging to the third century.

LIX. A small statue representing Paris.

CCXXXIX. A male bust, of the third century.

CCXXIX. Another male bust.

CCXXX. Bust of *Philetas,* formerly thought to be Seneca.
CCXXXIV. Statue of the *Emperor Commodus.* The head has been added.
CCXXVII. A seated statue, which has been given the head of *Mercury.* Nibby held it to be a figure of Apollo, but even the lyre is a reconstruction, and it is not possible to establish any sure indentification.
CCXXXII. Statue of a *Satyr,* in Parian marble. A reproduction of the one by Praxiteles.

The paintings:

167. LELIO ORSI (Novellara, 1511–1587), *St. Cecilia and St. Valerian* (canvas: 0,78 × 0,60). The attribution is due to Longhi, and was also confirmed at the recent Exhibition of Lelio Orsi's paintings in Reggio Emilia. Manilli, who mentions the picture as being among the first to be gathered in the Villa, writes that it was touched up by Domenichino. This might justify a certain academism, especially in the face of the saint.

398. TADDEO ZUCCARI (S. Angelo in Vado, 1529–1566), *The Dead Christ and Angels with Lighted Torches* (canvas: 2,32 × × 1,42). Vasari, who assigned the picture to Taddeo Zuccari, says that it was executed for the Farnese Cardinal, who intended it for Caprarola; but that Taddeo's brother, Frederico, had it, and at his death it passed to the Vitelleschi Family, who appear to have kept it until 1760. However in 1650 Manilli mentions it as being among the Borghese possessions, and described it as " a Pietà with four standing angels „.

322. MICHELE DI RODOLFO (Michele Tosini. Florence, 1503–1577), *Lucretia* (wood: 0,73 × 0,51).

323. MICHELE DI RODOLFO (Michele Tosini. Florence, 1503–1577), *Leda* (wood: 0,76 × 0,54). Both were attributed to Vasari in the " Fidecommisso „ Inventory and in Venturi's Catalogue. Voss brought forward the name of Francesco Brina, Gamba that of Michele di Ridolfo, which was also accepted by Longhi. The Tuscan characteristics of the two panels are evident. They must have belonged to a series of figures, perhaps allegorical ones, because others have appeared on the market.

33. GUY FRANÇOIS (Le Puy-en-Velay, 1578–1650 ca.), *The Judgement of Solomon* (canvas: 1,58 × 2). Attributed to several of Caravaggio's followers but assigned to Guy François by Longhi on the basis of a convincing comparison with a figure of St. Matthew in the Gavotti Collection, and with a signed picture at Le Puy, in Alvernia. However, on a recent occasion, Longhi preferred to allude to the artist as the " anonymous

master of the Judgement of Solomon „. The " stagy „ effect, and the dramatic posture of the figures on the extreme right of the picture are striking, and representative of a particular aspect of French painting, especially characteristc of those masters imbued with classicism who worked in Rome at the beginning of the seventeenth century.

27. GERARD HONTHORST (Utrecht, 1592–1662), *Susanna and the Elders* (canvas: 1,57 × 2,13). Signed and dated: G. Honthorst 1655. It is a typical example of the painting of this master, characterized by its sharp colouring and the elaborate manipulation of movement and expression.

148. FRENCH SCHOOL OF CARAVAGGIO (first half of the seventeenth century), *Joseph Interpreting the Dreams of the Prisoners* (canvas: 1,57 × 2,70). This picture, which was attributed to Valentin (Venturi), to Artemisia Gentileschi, an thend to Nicholas Renier (Longhi), is still surrounded by anonymous obscurity. Its dramatic action, bordering on the theatrical, suggests some French master.

271. GIORGIO VASARI (Arezzo, 1512–1574), *The Nativity* (wood: 1,11 × 0,72). Painted by Vasari for Pierantonio Bandini (Voss) and mentioned by Manilli in 1650 as being among the pictures of the Borghese Gallery. An interesting piece of work by the famous historian of Italian art.

404. GIROLAMO MUZIANO (?) (Acquafredda, 1528–1592), *St. Jerome* (canvas: 0,97 × 0,67). Longhi, like Cantalamessa before him, assigned this painting to Muziano, and even notices an affinity with the Flemish painter Wenceslas Coeberger.

2. ORAZIO BORGIANNI (died in 1616), *David with the Head of Goliath* (canvas: 2,02 × 1,12). It went under the name of Caravaggio, owing to its having been confused in the ancient inventories with a picture painted by this artist which is today exhibited in the Lanfranco Hall. Its restitution to Borgiani, due to Roberto Longhi, was accepted by Cantalamessa. Although it does not possess the fresh inspiration of the master, this picture appears to be directly influenced by him, and is remarkable for the solidity of its forms and the effect of intense light.

28. DIRK VAN BABUREN (Utrecht, heard of until about 1623), *The Taking of Christ* (canvas: 1,39 × 2,02). Formerly attributed to Manfredi. Then assigned by Fokker to David de Haen, Dirk van Baburen's assistant; and by Longhi to Baburen himself. All the attributions in the nineteenth–century inventories of the Gallery, centre round this name, which seems to stand out among Caravaggio's foreign followers. It is a forceful piece of painting, severely restrained and dramatic in effect.

464. PIERIN DEL VAGA (?) (Pietro Bonaccorsi. Florence, 1500–1547), *The Holy Family* (wood: 0,90 × 0,69). In the

Albertina Collection in Vienna, there is a drawing for this picture assigned to Luca Penni. Both Venturi and Longhi discarded Morelli's attribution to Pierin del Vaga, but it is a charming painting and, although of no great importance, may well be included among the works of this delicate artist.

31. GERARD HONTHORST (Utrecht, 1592–1662), *A Concert* (canvas: 1,68 × 2,20). Attributed to Rombauts by Morelli, then to Gerard Honthorst by Bode and Venturi. Aldo de Rinaldis thinks this Dutch artist must have painted it in Rome while he was more under the influence of Saraceni than of Caravaggio.

191. LUCA CAMBIASO (Moneglia 1527–1585), *Cupid* (canvas: 0,90 × 0,78).

FIRST FLOOR

ENTRANCE

246. SASSOFERRATO (Giovan Battista Salvi. Sassoferrato, 1609–1685), *The Three Ages of Man* (canvas: 0,94 × 1,57). This is a copy of a picture of the same subject by Titian in the Bridgewater Collection in London. The three ages are represented by a group of little children on the right, a couple of young lovers in the foreground, and an old man in the middle distance surrounded by skulls, upon which he is gazing in a melancholy manner, while sheep graze in the background.

3. SCHOOL OF BASSANO (sixteenth century), *A country scene or an allegory of Spring* (canvas: 1,10 × 1,46).

29. SCHOOL OF BASSANO (sixteenth century), *A country scene or an allegory of Winter* (canvas: 1,10 × 1,46).

4. RUTILIO MANETTI (Siena, 1571–1639), *Andromeda Bound to the Rock* (canvas: 1,75 × 1,18). This painting, which was formerly attributed to the Cavalier d'Arpino, was recognized by Voss as being the work of Rutilio Manetti, from an engraving by Bernardino Capitelli.

123. LUCA CAMBIASO (Moneglia, 1527–1585), *Venus on the Sea with Cupid* (canvas: 1,18 × 1,10). A decorative picture, fresh and pleasing in the clear tones and airy atmosphere that surround the figure of Venus.

10. JACOPO ZUCCHI (Florence, 1542–1590), *Cupid and Psyche* (canvas: 1,80 × 1,35). Signed and dated: Jac. F. Zuc. Fac. 1589.

ANTON DE MARON (Vienna, 1733–Rome, 1797) painted the ceiling, between 1784 and 1786, with five episodes from the story of *Aeneas and Dido*. In the centre, almost as an apotheosis, is the *Death of Dido*, and round it: *Aeneas fleeing from Troy with his father Anchises* — a subject often repeated in this Gallery —, *the meeting of Aeneas and Dido*, *Aeneas at the banquet given by Dido*, *Aeneas exhorted by Mercury to continue his journey*.

VINCENZO PACETTI (Castelbolognese, 1746 ca.–1820) sculptured the very fine white marble fireplace, with amethyst inlay and bronze ornamentations. A red marble bas–relief surrounded by green porphyry, set in the centre, represents *Boreas bearing away Orithyia*. The inner part of the fireplace is lined with majolica tiles with the dragon and the eagle, the symbols of the Borghese armorial bearings, on either side.

In the centre of the hall a large alabaster basin stands upon a base of white and antique green marble. The two tables, one of *breccia corallina*, and the other inlaid with various coloured marbles, belong to the eighteenth century. The doors, painted with simple ornamentations, in keeping with the style of decoration carried out at the time of Marcantonio Borghese, complete the ornamental scheme of the hall.

173. PIER FRANCESCO TOSCHI (Florence, 1502–1567), *Tobias and the Angel* (wood: 0,75 × 0,52). The attribution was put forward by Longhi. A comparison with the frescoes of Poggio alla Noce, published by O. H. Giglioli, leaves no dout as to the parentage of this picture, which stands apart from any other painting of the Florentine manneristic school owing to its sharp colouring and the solidity of the figures.

433. LORENZO DI CREDI (Florence, 1459–1537), *Madonna and Child with St. John* (wood: diam. 0,90). Though Lorenzo di Credi is not one of the greatest artists, he is a delicate and precise painter and, in this round where the composition devolves along the central axis, he reaches a high standard of execution, and there is a transparent tenderness in his figures. The obvious Flemish influence in the landscape, derived from Memling — as it were an echo of one of Leonardo's paintings, to whom the picture was once attributed — reappears in the melancholy expression of his gentle Madonna, and in the poetic care with which the pot of flowers is treated.

375. ANDREA DEL SARTO (Andrea d'Agnolo. Florence, 1486–1530), *A Predella with the Pietà and four Saints* (wood: 0,22 × 0,68). A youthful painting, carried out, according to Longhi, during the first ten years of the sixteenth century.

348. SANDRO BOTTICELLI (Alessandro Filipepi. Florence, 1445–1510), *Madonna and Child, St. John and Angels* (wood: diam. 1,70). Although not one of Sandro's most successful works, this round is so harmoniously carried out that it would be hard to distinguish more than one hand in it, or to consider it the product of his workshop. The circular composition arranges itself naturally round the figure of the Madonna bending over Her Child, and this affective movement broadens out and refracts in the gentle assent of the angels. Even the colouring, acting in conjunction with the movement, is subdued and subordinate to the essential function of the line.

439. FRA BARTOLOMEO DELLA PORTA (Baccio della Porta. Florence, 1475–1527), *The Holy Family* (wood: diam. 1,12). Although this picture was attributed to Lorenzo di Credi in all the Borghese inventories, and confirmed by Aldo de Rinaldis in the 1948 catalogue, Longhi's assignment of it to Fra Bartolomeo is convincing, owing to the deep shadows and the solidity of the figures, which is not in keeping with Credi's manner. The landscape and even the scheme of the composition are vaguely reminiscent of Leonardo. However Fra Bartolomeo's well defined personality is indisputable.

329. PIER FRANCESCO TOSCHI (Florence, 1502–1567), *The Judgement of Solomon* (wood: 0,67 × 0,52). This picture, which was attributed by Morelli to Piero di Cosimo, and by Venturi to his workshop, must also be referred to the Florentine painter Pier Francesco Toschi, who is here more academic than in his Tobias and the Angel. It can be seen from a similar painting in London, which belongs to A. Scharf, and represents the Death of the Laocoon, how both pictures are derived from Filippino Lippi's partially destroyed frescoes at Poggio a Cajano

314. VENTURA SALIMBENI (Siena, 1568–1613), *Madonna and Child* (wood: 0,30 × 0,20). The painter's signature, Ventura Salimbeni, is on the left. The correct paternity of this little panel had already been recognized by Longhi before the signature was discovered. Venturi drew attention to its connection with a drawing by Raphael in the Louvre.

369. RAFFAELLO SANZIO (Urbino, 1482–1520), *The Deposition* (wood: 1,84 × 1,76). Signed and dated: Raphael Urbinas M. D. VII. It was commissioned of Raphael in remembrance of Grifonetto Baglioni, who fell during the struggle for the mastery of Perugia, by Atalanta Baglioni, who wished her own sorrow to be portrayed in the grief of the Madonna. The predella of this panel, which was carried off during the night in order that it might be secured for Scipione Borghese's collection, is in the Vatican Picture Gallery; the top, which was however done by assistants, is in the Picture Gallery of Perugia.

The painting has a certain academic emphasis which detracts from the emotional effect, but the figure of the Magdalene, the head of Christ, the distant landscape and the clear sky are passages of sincere poetic beauty.

232. SANTI DI TITO (Borgo San Sepolcro, 1536–1603), *Madonna and Child* (canvas: 0,33 × 0,28). A delicate little picture, both as regards composition and colouring, where the shading has a slightly iridescent sheen.

397. RAFFAELLO SANZIO (Urbino, 1483–1520), *Portrait of a Man* (canvas: 0,45 × 0,39). This picture, which was formerly attributed to Holbein, and then to Perugino whose portrait is was supposed to be, was recognized as being by Raphael by Morelli, who reaffirmed the ancient attribution of the 1765 inventory. The vigorous portrait, from which a fur cap, curiously added at some unknown period, was removed when it was restored in 1911, still shows Umbrian characteristics and a certain similarity to Flemish portraiture, which place it before Raphael's Roman period, and date it to about 1502.

371. RAFFAELLO SANZIO (Urbino, 1483–1520), *Portrait of a Lady with a Unicorn* (wood: 0,65 × 0,51). The picture represented a figure of St. Catherine, but Cantalamessa perceived the cloak, the hands, the martyr's wheel and palm were by a different hand; and when it was restored in 1935, after Longhi had ascertained its attribution to Raphael, and a radiographic examination revealed the repainted parts, a more lyrical and extensive landscape appeared behind the figure which, instead of a wheel, was found to be holding a Unicorn, the symbol of chastity.

Though erroneously thought to be Maddalena Doni, the portrait can be compared with a drawing by Raphael in the Louvre. The soft green of the costume, the pomegranate red of the velvet, and the grace and noble bearing of the figure, leave no doubt as to the parentage of the picture.

401. PIETRO PERUGINO (?) (Pietro Vannucci. Città della Pieve, 1450–1523), *Madonna and Child* (wood: 0,45 × 0,37). Adolfo Venturi queried the attribution, but it was again brought forward by Longhi and accepted by Aldo de Rinaldis. The painting is delicate, and the landscape and image of the Madonna and Child have the charm of signed works by this master. However the colouring, which has a reddish foundation, would rather point to a disciple.

377. PINTORICCHIO (Bernardino di Betto. Perugia, 1454–1513), *The Crucifixion, with Sts. Jerome and Christopher* (wood: 0,50 × 0,40). Every detail of the landscape, which is painted with the delicate grace of an illuminator, performs a decorative function: the tall, slim cross; the flowering stick on which St. Christopher leans; the elegant bushes; the slow, twining river. Venturi

thinks it was a small portable altarpiece. It has been preserved with its original frame which is in almost perfect condition.

343. PIERO DI COSIMO Florence, 1462–1521), *Madonna and Child with St. John and Angels Playing Musical Instruments* (wood: diam. 1,40). A charming, elegant picture in spite of its spectral appearance. It was apparently never finished, but its very incompleteness seems to render the figures of the angels more immaterial, and that of the Madonna bending towards her Child more ethereal and unreal.

421. MARIOTTO ALBERTINELLI (Florence, 1474–1515), *The Saviour* (wood: 0,60 × 0,54). The details of this panel, which was formerly attributed to Perugino and assigned to Albertinelli by Adolfo Venturi, are finely painted, especially in the landscape which shows a combination of Umbrian and Tuscan motives.

ROOM X

The Labours of Hercules were painted on the ceiling in 1786 by CHRISTOPHER UNTERBERGHER (Cavalese, 1732–1798), who represented the *Apotheosis* in the centre, with *Hercules in the Garden of the Hesperides; Hercules pursuing the Centaur Nessus, the seducer of Dejaneira; Hercules killing Licas,* and *Hercules dying on the pyre,* round it. The decorative motives are by GIOVAN BATTISTA MARCHETTI.

In the centre of the room:

CCLXIII. TIBURZIO VERGELLI (Camerino, 1555–1610), *The Gipsy Girl*. Recomposed from an ancient fragment and rivetted with grey marble and bronze ornamentations. Venturi attributed this reconstruction to Vergelli, though Aldo de Rinaldis considered it to be by Nicolò Cordier.

The fireplace of white marble and red porphyry was done by VINCENZO PACETTI. The doors painted with folklore scenes are by THADDEUS KUNTZE (1730 ca.–1793). Against the entrance wall is a grey marble table with gilt bronze decorations, belonging to the eighteenth century.

294. SCHOOL OF RAPHAEL, *The Archers.*
300. *Offerings to Vertumnus and Pomona.*
303. *The Marriage of Alexander and Roxana.*

These three much damaged and restored frescoes were removed in 1834 from the so-called Casino di Raffaello which stood in the Borghese Gardens and was pulled down in 1848. In all probability they belong to the School of Raphael, and show a decided feeling for decoration, especially in the fragment representing the Archers.

461. ANDREA SOLARIO (active between 1495 and 1522), *Christ Bearing the Cross* (wood: 0,58 × 0,67). The signature and date at the back: Andrea de Solario Pinxit 1511, does not seem to be authentic. However the attribution to Solario remains unaltered. The leaden colouring and the engraved outlines of this picture are reminiscent of Flemish art, and indeed it seems likely that it was painted under the influence of this school when Solario passed through Flanders, and perhaps stopped at Antwerp, on his way back from Gaillon.

462. SODOMA (Giovan Antonio Bazzi. Vercelli, 1477–1549), *Pietà* (wood: 0,69 × 0,58). This picture belonged to Scipione Borghese's collection right from its foundation, and Manilli mentioned it in 1650 as being attributed by some to Sodoma, and by others to Leonardo. Although darkened by a thick coating of varnish, the vigorous dramatic sense of the painting is still evident.

408. SALVIATI FRANCESCO (Francesco de' Rossi. Florence, 1510–1563), *Portrait of Cardinal Marcello Cervini degli Spannocchi* (wood: 1,03 × 0,86). Although the scheme is in the grandiose style of Raphael the composition remains refined and elegant, and the same can be said of the colouring which keeps to a potential scale of old rose and dull red. The attribution to Salviati is due to Aldo de Rinaldis, who dates the portrait to somewhere around 1548.

459. SODOMA (Giovan Antonio Bazzi. Vercelli, 1477–1549), *The Holy Family* (wood: 0,75 × 0,67). Here the characteristics and style of this Sienese artist appear to be a combination of Leonardo's precepts, and of the Tuscan and even of Raphael's manner of painting. The colouring is subdued, in dull blue–green tones, but the face of the Blessed Virgin is of a soft delicacy, and the patch of landscape remains vital and poetic.

422. MARCELLO VENUSTI (Mantova, 1512 ca.–1579), *Pietà* (wood: 0,56 × 0,40). The composition, which is taken from a drawing by Michael Angelo, still keeps the grandeur and nobility of the original design, and Venusti must have based his panel on this rather than on the print of it by Bonasone.

335. ALONSO BERRUGUETE (Parades Nava, 1486–1521), *Madonna, with Child, St. John and St. Elizabeth* (wood: 1,12×0,90). The very bad preservation of this painting makes its attribution, with wavers between Fra' Bartolomeo (Venturi), Piero di Cosimo (Berenson) and Pontormo (Longhi) all the more difficult and doubtful. But the last studies of Longhi have enabled to recognize in it a true work of Alonso Berruguete.

88. ANDREA DEL BRESCIANINO (Andrea di Giovanni Antonio da Brescia, active in Siena between 1507 and 1525), *Portrait*

of a Young Woman with the Symbols of St. Catherine (wood: 0,40×0,28). A now undoubted painting by this sixteenth–century academician, who has succeeded in keeping his own elegant and pleasing individuality, decided colouring, and clever drawing.

334. ANDREA DEL SARTO (Andrea d'Agnolo. Florence, 1486–1531), *Madonna and Child with St. John* (wood: 1,54 × 1,01). Above, in the centre of the composition, is the artists monogram. He must have painted this picture around 1514, when he came most strongly under the influence of Michael Angelo. The freedom of the composition, the supple movement, the stupendous equilibrium of the parts, the colouring which, in spite of its being spoilt by repeated repair, is of real creative significance, are truly magnificent.

399. RIDOLFO DEL GHIRLANDAIO (Florence, 1482–still active in 1561), *Portrait of a Young Man* (wood: 0,47 × 0,26). Formerly, though for no particular reason, thought to be a portrait of Raphael. Cavalcaselle attributes it to Ridolfo del Ghirlandaio, whose rather affected grace and brilliant colouring it certainly shows.

456. GIAMPIETRINO (Giovanni Pietro Rizzo, or Giovanni Pedrini. Sixteenth century), the *Madonna Feeding her Child* (wood: 0,78 × 0,60). This panel, which was mentioned in a catalogue of the Borghese collection as early as 1760, is obviously derived from the school of Leonardo. Its persistently gentle accent, and the luminous smile make the figure of the Blessed Virgin a graceful accomplishment. A copy, with variations, is mentioned by Venturi in the State Gallery of Munich.

324. ANDREA DEL BRESCIANINO (Andrea di Giovanni Antonio da Brescia, active in Siena between 1507 and 1525), *Venus with two Cupids* (wood: 1,68 × 0,67). In his description of 1650 Manilli mentions " two long narrow pictures of Venus, the first thought to be by Andrea del Sarto, and the second, which is very finely finished, is in the German style „. Though the second is identifiable with the Venus by Cranach, the first certainly refers to this picture which Frizzoni attributes to Andrea del Brescianino. The colour of the niche, which is composed of grey on grey, is laid on by an able hand, and the whole, though confined to a cold treatment which makes the figure like a statue, has that vague romantic atmosphere proper to the followers of Andrea del Sarto.

435. MARCO D'OGGIONO (Oggiono, 1470 ca.–1530), *The Redeemer in the Act of Blessing* (wood: 0,33 × 0,26). This little picture was attributed to Leonardo ever since it was given to Cardinal Scipione Borghese by Paul V in 1611. The Pope thought a lot of it, and it hung in his bedroom. The new, more correct attribution is due to Gustavo Frizzoni.

514. THE MASTER OF THE SFORZESCA ALTARPIECE (an anonymous Lombard of the sixteenth century), *Head of a Woman* (a silverpoint drawing gone over in pencil, on paper, 0,18×0,24). A comparison with the head of the Madonna in the so-called Sforzesca Altarpiece in the Brera, attributed to a follower of Leonardo, immediatly suggested Jacobsen's assignation of this head to the same master, and would seem to be a more fitting definition of the artist who, in the old inventories, was mistaken for Leonardo himself.

115. BERNARDINO LICINIO (Pordenone, 1489 ca.-1516), *Portrait of the Artist's Brother and his Family* (canvas: 1,18×1,65). Signed: B. Lycinii opus, at the end of a long inscription which says: " Exprimit hic fratem tota cum gente Lycinus et vitam his forma prorogat arte sibi ,,. It is more interesting as a document of the costumes of the period, than as a real work of art.

281. BERNARD STRIEGEL (Memmingen, 1461-1528), *Portrait of Charles V* (wood: 0,42 × 0,22). Leo van Puyvelde thinks this portrait is more likely to be the brother of Charles V who was also invested with the Order of the Golden Fleece. On the cap is a medallion with an image of the Blessed Virgin and the invocation: " O. Mater Dei. Memento mei ,,. The picture can be dated to about 1519, and is a typical example of German portraiture of that period.

287. ALBRECHT DÜRER (Nuremberg, 1471-1528), *Portrait of a Man* (wood: 0,36 × 0,26). At the top, on the background is the date 1505, which for some reason Venturi supposes to be apocryphal. In the " Fidecommisso ,, List of 1833 it was attributed to Holbein, but restored to Dürer by Waagen (who took it for a portrait of Wilhelm Pirkheimer) and by Longhi and Benesch. This was also accepted by Aldo de Rinaldis, with a few reservations. It is excellently painted and a vivid psychological study.

326. LUCAS CRANACH (Lucas Sunders. Cranach, 1472-1533), *Venus and Cupid with a Honeycomb* (wood: 1,70 × 0,73). In 1509 Lucas Cranach the Elder painted a picture with Venus and Cupid (today at the Hermitage of Leningrad) which can be considered the prototype of all the later variations of the theme, and which is also carried out in the panel of the Borghese Gallery. The date 1531 appears to be false, and the artists monogram with a winged dragon, on the trunk of the tree, was partly repainted during an ancient restoration. But there is no doubt about its attribution to this German artist, and his Venus, bathed in moonlight, introduces an unusual northern note into Cardinal Scipione's collection.

328. DOMENICO PULIGO (Florence, 1475-1527), *Mary Magdalene* (wood: 0,58 × 0,41). The noble atmosphere of

the picture has induced certain critics, such as Venturi and de Rinaldis, to consider it to have been painted by Andrea del Sarto. It is however the work of Puligo, who interprets the romanticism of the master in a softer climate, and with a more vaporous movement, where outlines disappear.

444. ANGELO BRONZINO (Agnolo di Cosimo. Florence, 1503–1572), *St. John the Baptist* (wood: 1,20 × 0,92). Signed: Bronzino Flor. It belongs to the artist's early manner and has the sharp form and crude colouring characteristic of a youthful work. The figure rises in monumental relief, out of proportion with the rest of the picture, and the effort with which it bends in diagonals and intersecting surfaces, contrary to all the laws of dynamics, makes it a laboured and academic composition.

332. ROSSO FIORENTINO (Giovan Battista Rosso. Florence, 1494–1540), *Madonna and Child, with St. Joseph and St. John* (wood: 0,64 × 0,40). The agitated, individual style of this very personal artist, who painted under the influence of Florentine mannerism, is extremely modern in feeling. In this unfinished panel, the creative force is emphasized by the two groups where the embrace is repeated in inverted formation while the landscape is focused in a poetic distance which is however treated analytically in every detail of its construction.

ROOM XI

The ceiling of this room, like the two small rooms that lead out of it, belongs to the latest restoration of the Villa, when Francesco Borghese arranged the Museum in it. The fireplace, with decorative majolica tiles, dates back to the eighteenth century, and has bronze ornamentations in Empire style.

292. JACOPO ZUCCHI (Florence, 1542 ca.–1590), *Treasures of the Sea* (copper: 0,53 × 0,45). Baglione mentions this picture, under the title of " Coral Fishing „ , as having been painted by Zucchi for Cardinal de' Medici, during the first years of his stay in Rome. But this reference was forgotten, and the picture was then attributed to Poelemburg, and also, probably owing to a confusion in the names, to Zuccari, as well as to Lavinia Fontana. Voss restored it to Zucchi. It is quite likely that this gay fabulous representation was in some way connected with the recent discovery of America.

293. JACOPO ZUCCHI (Florence, 1542 ca.–1590), *An Allegory of Creation* (copper: 0,50 × 0,30). It was identified by Longhi as being the work of Jacopo Zucchi, and is similar to the aforegoing picture in its elaborate anecdotal manner, which justifies

its having been thought to belong to the Flemish school. In fact it was assigned to Breughel.

77. NICOLÒ DELL'ABATE (Modena, 1509 ca.–1571), *Portrait of a Woman* (parchment: 0,45 × 0,30). This portrait, carried out with great simplicity and dignity, according to the precepts of Emilian painting, was attributed to Nicolò dell'Abate by Carlo Gamba. The figure is sedate and well dressed, though without ostentation; and its modest, almost rustic bearing immediately arouses sympathy. The same can be said of the colouring, which keeps to slightly golden brown tints.

547. GIROLAMO SAVOLDO (Brescia, 1480 ca.–1548), *Tobias and the Angel* (canvas: 1,26 × 0,96). Bought in 1908 for ten thousand lire, owing to the insistence of Giulio Cantalamessa who claimed the excellent quality of the painting and, contrary to general opinion, attributed it to Savoldo. It is a clever romantic picture, in the particular manner of this artist born on the borders of Venice and Lombardy. The vivid luminous figure of the Angel stands out in the composition as a thing by itself, while the light softens the colours — silver–grey and velvet-red — and the face becomes spiritualized and transparent.

193. LORENZO LOTTO (Venice, 1480–1556), *Holy Conversation* (wood: 0,67 × 0,73). Signed and dated: Laurent. Lotus M. D. VIII. The artist was twenty–eight when he painted this panel. He was then influenced by Dürer who had just finished a picture of Jesus Disputing with the Doctors, in Venice, from which the figure of St. Onuphrius is derived. The suggestion of German painting is also noticeable in the sharp outline to the colours, where crude reds, clashing greens and glittering whites are boldly combined. The painter's fanciful originality is expressed in the device of an open heart, with Christ's monogram in the wound, which the Bishop is offering the Child: and the eagerness with which the Child reaches out to take it was later repeated in the Holy Conversation formerly at the Quirinal, and today in the Gallery of Ancient Art in Rome.

186. ANTONIO PALMA (Serinalta, 1550, and still active in 1575), *The Return of the Prodigal Son* (canvas: 1,10 × 2,02). Formerly attributed to Bonifacio Veneziano. Though it is obviously the work of a secondary painter, there is still a sense of proportion in the composition and in the blending of the colours, which makes it a worthy representative of the great Venetian school of painting.

430. BARTOLOMEO MONTAGNA (Orzinuovi, 1450–1523), *The Young Christ* (wood: 0,24 × 0,20). Part of a larger composition which according to Longhi, must have been painted about 1500. It was attributed to Timoteo Viti, and then to the Flo-

rentine school. Although the quality of the painting is not very good, it is an interesting picture in keeping with the style of this Venetian artist.

164. GIOVANNI CARIANI (Giovanni Busi. Bergamo, 1480–1541), *Holy Conversation* (canvas: 0,73 × 0,94). Obviously influenced by Titian and Palma the Elder. Here Cariani shows himself to be a sincere adherent of this great school of painting, and this Holy Conversation is one of his most representative pictures.

185. LORENZO LOTTO (Venice, 1480–1556), *Portrait by himself* (canvas: 1,18 × 1,05). Black dominates in this portrait, accentuating the paleness of the hands, the sombre melancholy face, and the romantic note supplied by the fallen rose petals amongst which a small skull is hidden. The landscape seen in the background accompanies the resigned, rather sad figure, in subdued tones. Here is a very different picture from the Holy Conversation (No. 193), revealing another of the many sides of this versatile and surprising artist.

163. JACOPO PALMA THE ELDER (Serinalta, 1480–1528), *Madonna and Child with Saints and a Devout Person* (wood: 0,71 × 1,08). A brilliantly coloured picture, where each surface is marked by a very definite patch of colour, rather than by the outline. It was probably painted about 1512, and showr Palma to be still under provincial influences; however broades Venetian traits begin to appear spontaneously. The portrait of the devout person with folded hands, is one of the finest examples of sixteenth–century Venetian portraiture.

139. GIROLAMO SAVOLDO (Brescia, 1480 ca.–1548), *A study for a portrait* (canvas: 0,60 × 0,40). Here too the romantic element of Savoldo's art is most in evidence, and calls to mind some of Caravaggio's early work. The painting is carried out on a warm foundation, with a light massing of the colour, and in a languid tone which determines its atmosphere. The exceedingly deep colouring plays upon the reflections of the whites, the tawny hair and tunic, and the soft graduation of the shadows leading from one surface to another.

38, 47, 296, 299. GRIMALDI G. F. (Bologna, 1606–1680 ca.), *Four Landscapes.*

ROOM XII

357. SIMONE CANTARINI (Pesaro, 1612–1648), *St. John the Baptist in the Desert* (canvas: 0,45 × 0,60). The attribution to Cantarini was confirmed by Longhi. It is a small decorative picture that the artist has treated lightly.

83. ANNIBALE CARRACCI (Bologna, 1560–1609), *Head of a Laughing Youth* (paper backed with canvas: 0,45×0,28). This laughingh head, wearing a buffoon's cap, is sketched in rapidly and easily with charcoal leaving vigorous and surprisingly agile outlines. It shows the free atmosphere in which the Carraccis moved apart from any academic rule, which, above all, was of a controversial nature, in opposition to the realistic innovations introduced by Caravaggio.

382. SASSOFERRATO (Giovanni Battista Salvi. Sassoferrato, 1609–1685), *Madonna and Child* (canvas: 0,73 × 0,62). Bought for the Borghese collection in 1818. It is a free copy of one of Raphael's schemes and bears witness of the mannerism and affectation to be found even in the painting of the great Urbino master.

81. LAVINIA FONTANA (Bologna, 1552–1614), *A Youthful Portrait* (canvas: 0,40 × 0,37). Signed and dated: Lavi.a Fon.a F. 1606. Lavinia was then in Rome, and her regard for Raphael is in fact evident.

560. SEBASTIANO CONCA (Gaeta, 1680–1764), *Madonna and Child with St. John Nepomux* (canvas: 1,03 × 0,69). There is a drawing of this picture, which Longhi identified as certainly being by Conca, in the Gabinetto Nazionale delle Stampe at the Farnesina, as well as an engraving in the Borghese Gallery itself (storage).

507. PASQUALE OTTINI (Verona, 1580–1630), *The Resurrection of Lazarus* (slate: 0,46 × 0,36). Identified by Longhi on the comparison with the Assumption of the Blessed Virgin Mary at Vanzo, and with the paintings in the Pellegrini Chapel in S. Bernardino at Verona. There is an attempt, in this picture, at strong contrasts of light and shade, bearing witness of Caravaggio's influence even in the distant Veronese territory.

437. LAVINIA FONTANA (Bologna, 1552–1614), *The Infant Jesus Asleep* (copper: 0,45 × 0,37). In spite of the laborious affectation of the composition, this is a pleasing picture and one of the best by this Emilian painter.

55. DOMENICHINO (Domenico Zampieri. Bologna, 1581–1641), *A Sibyl* (canvas: 1,23 × 0,94). Painted for Cardinal Scipione Borghese, and mentioned by Bellori. It has been interpreted as a Muse, an Allegory of Music, St. Cecilia and the Sibyl of Cumae. Though it certainly represents a Sibyl, it must be admitted there is an obvious reference to music in the scroll of music the young woman is holding, and in the large viola seen in the background.

231. CAVALIER D'ARPINO (Giuseppe Cesari. Arpino, 1568–1640), *The Flight into Egypt* (copper: 0,45 × 0,33). One of the

most pleasing works by this artist who, in his smaller paintings, acquires grace and harmony which is too often lost in his larger compositions where his manneristic and laborious efforts are apparent.

431. MARCANTONIO BASSETTI (Verona, 1588–1630), *Christ Taken from the Cross* (canvas: 0,48 × 0,36). Bassetti belongs, with Turchi and Ottini, to that group of Veronese seventeenth-century artists whose separate personalities were individuated by Longhi. In this small picture, which was formerly attributed to Tiarini, the artist has combined the Venetian love of colour with Caravaggio's new style of painting which was widely diffused in the province.

527. RUTILIO MANETTI (?) (Siena, 1571–1639), *The Three Graces* (canvas: 0,33 × 0,38). Voss is responsible for the attribution to Manetti, but it is not altogether convincing. In the inventory list it was assigned to the Sienese Francesco Vanni. The characteristics of this provincial school of painting are evident in the trite and affected little figures memorized from Raphael's group in the Museum of Chantilly.

318. CARLO DOLCI (Florence, 1616–1686), *Madonna and Child* (canvas: 0,86 × 0,71). Dolci, who is an easy composer, careful and precise in his drawing and colouring, paints a pleasant group, without however succeeding in giving it any real artistic value.

460. BARTOLOMEO PASSAROTTI (Bologna, 1529–1592), *A Lesson in Anatomy* (canvas: 0,42 × 0,52). Formerly attributed to Lucio Massari, one of Passarotti's pupils, but Longhi thought it more likely to be the work of the master. It is a scene that might have appealed to a Flemish painter, and is indeed derived from that school which was then widespread in Italian art.

549. SIMONE CANTARINI (Pesaro, 1612–1648), *The Holy Family* (canvas: 0,96 × 0,73). Bought in 1912 at the instigation of Corrado Ricci who was the first to recognize it as the work of Cantarini, and published by Cantalamessa who mentions it as an example of this painter's creative freedom in comparison with Reni, whom he followed.

515. ANNIBALE CARRACCI (Bologna, 1560–1609), *Jupiter and Juno* (wood: 0,33 × 0,39). Annibale took this little scene, so Longhi points out, from the large frescoes of Palazzo Farnese, making a few changes in the details.

542. POMPEO BATONI (Lucca, 1708–1787), *Madonna and Child* (canvas: 0,64 × 0,48). Added to the Gallery in 1912, and published for the first time by d'Achiardi. I is a charming composition, completely eighteenth-century in style, with clear sparkling colours that can still be enjoyed today in spite of the many cracks.

378. CAVALIER D'ARPINO (Giuseppe Cesari. Arpino, 1568–1640), *The Rape of Europe* (wood: 0,58 × 0,45). Here too the Cavalier d'Arpino composes his figures with rare freshness and imagination.

364. PIETRO DA CORTONA (Pietro Berettini. Cortona, 1596–1669), *Portrait of Marcello Sacchetti* (canvas: 1,52 × 1,37). This painting, which is carried out on the lines of Flemish portraiture, is remarkable for the solidity of the figure which stands out against a neutral background, and for the vivid rendering of the strong features. The marked decorative sense, which is always present in this artist, appears in the care with which the ornamental motives of the table are treated, where Pietro da Cortona's ability as an architect is brought out in the force of the projections and in the plastic relief of the caryatid. The identification of the figure, which was formerly thought to be Giuseppe Ghisleri, is due to Giovanni Incisa della Rocchetta.

ROOM XIII

374. GIULIO ROMANO (Giulio Pippi. Rome, 1492–1546), *The Blessed Virgin with St. John who is Handing a Small Bird to Jesus* (wood: 1,16 × 0,90). In the " Fidecommisso ,, List, this composition, of which Annibale Carracci made an etching, was attributed to Raphael. Its derivation from this master is indeed evident in the type of the figures of the Madonna, the Infant Jesus and St. John; but the originality of the painting is in the colouring, and in certain devices, such as the chair with unusual, animated legs, all of which points to a very definite personality, like that of Giulio Pippi, called Giulio Romano.

80. SCIPIONE PULZONE (Gaeta, 1550–1595), *Portrait of a Lady* (wood: 0,72 × 0,56). The serious expression of this portrait, which is analytic in the decorative details of the costume and jewellery, is unusual and striking.

320. GIULIO ROMANO (?) (Giulio Pippi. Rome, 1492–1546), *Madonna and Child with St. John* (wood: 1,25 × 0,86). The attribution is much questioned, but it is obviously derived from Giulio Romano whose constructive solidity it preserves. Its " stupendous marmoreal ,, style of painting caused Longhi to be in favour of some Florentine master.

415. PELLEGRINO TIBALDI (Valsolda, 1522–1581), *Adoration of the Holy Child* (canvas: 1,57 × 1,05). Signed and dated: Peregrinus Tibaldi Bonon. faciebat. Anno Aetatis MDXLVIIII. This great decorator of Bolognese palaces composes in Michael Angelo's grandiose style.

412. ROMAN SCHOOL (XVIth century), *The Holy Family, St. John and St. Elyzabeth* (canvas: 1,39×1,12).

496. GUGLIELMO DELLA PORTA (?) (born at Porlezza, died in Rome in 1577), *The Crucifixion*. The ancient inventories attributed this wax bas–relief in a jasper shrine to Michael Angelo. Aldo de Rinaldis considered it to be of Flemish workmanship.

313. SCIPIONE PULZONE (Gaeta, 1550 ca.–1595), *The Holy Family* (canvas: 1,35 × 1,05). The cold colouring, confined to sharp calculated outlines, divides the painting of this diligent mannerist into surfaces, almost as thought it were an inlay; and only in his portraits does he succeed in representing life with any degree of intensity.

468. DOMENICO PULIGO (Florence, 1492–1527), *Madonna and Child with Two Angels* (wood: diam. 0,78). The blurred colouring, in the manner of Andrea del Sarto, is characteristic of this painter who concentrates on the faces and treats the draperies with less intensity.

463. BACHIACCA (Francesco Ubertini. Florence, 1490–1557), *The Story of Joseph* (wood: 0,78 × 1,80). Morelli assigned this panel to Bachiacca, and both Venturi and Longhi accepted his conclusions. The same episodes which the painter represented in the smaller panels under Nos. 425–427 and 440–442, are here united in one composition, and the same rose–yellow iridescence and almost the same figures are repeated, which confirms the identity of the hand. Here more space is given to the broad landscape. This panel may also have been part of a painted chest.

425–427. BACHIACCA (Francesco Ubertini. Florence, 1490–1557), *The Story of Joseph* (originally on wood, transferred to canvas: 0,26 × 0,14). Two incidents in the story of Joseph are recounted: Joseph sold by his brothers, and the arrest of Joseph's brothers. The small size of the panels suggests they may have been used in the decoration of a chest or cupboard.

432. DOMENICO PULIGO (Florence, 1492–1527), *The Holy Family* (wood: 0,74 × 0,54). There are several contemporary copies of this little picture, suggesting their derivation from an original, perhaps by Andrea del Sarto himself, which was copied by his followers.

440–442. BACHIACCA (Francesco Ubertini. Florence, 1490–1557), *The Story of Joseph* (wood: 0,26 × 0,14). Other two incidents in the aforegoing series: the search for the stolen cup, and the finding of the cup in Benjamin's sack.

458. FRANCIABIGIO (Francesco di Cristoforo. Florence, 1482-1524), *Madonna and Child with St. John*. Longhi dates it to about 1518. Here too the influence of Andrea del Sarto is noticeable.

ROOM XIV

This hall takes its name from GIOVANNI LANFRANCO (Parma, 1582-1647) who frescoed the ceiling of the great loggia giving onto the gardens. A feigned monochrome perspective leads up to the caryatids that support the great central frame in which the painter represented the *Gods on Olympus*. In 1786 DOMENICO CORVI (Viterbo, 1721-1803) closed the Loggia and carried out a radical restoration, which modified the original fresco, especially in its colouring. However the painting as a whole is still imposing and harmonious, and provides a living testimony of the decorative ability of the artists that gathered round the Carracci family.

CCLVI. A small seventeenth–century vase.

35-40-44-49. FRANCESCO ALBANI (Bologna, 1578-1660), *Stories of Love* (canvas: diam. 1,54). Four large rounds, entitl-Historia ed " d'Amore ", painted by Albani in Rome, about 1625. The four episodes are represented against a pleasant landscape: 1) Venus in Vulcan's forge, where little Cupids are pointing arrows, and Diana meditates revenge for the death of Hippolytus. 2) Venus at her toilette, surrounded by Nymphs and Cupids. 3) Adonis hunting the boar, and the jealous Mars pointing him out to Diana, who is about to let fly her arrows. 4) Diana causing the Nymphs to disarm the Cupids and destroy their weapons. The enormous success of these rounds directly they appeared, and their eminent suitability for decorative purposes, brought the artist numerous orders for copies. Albani is known to have painted them for Cardinal Maurice of Savoy, the Count of Carouge, and Ferdinand Gonzaga (Venturi).

36. ALESSANDRO TIARINI (Bologna, 1577-1668), *Rinaldo and Armida* (canvas: 1,24 × 1,85). This episode taken from Orlando Furioso is told by Tiarini by means of those " difficult foreshortenings ", commended by Malvasia in connection with this picture. Manilli also mentions it in the Borghese collection. Here the artist has reached an intensity of both dramatic and decorative effect which must have impressed his contemporaries, for it was widely imitated.

67. GIOVANNI LANFRANCO (Parma, 1582-1647), *Joseph and the Wife of Potiphar* (canvas: 1,10-1,57). Though poor from

a pictorial point of view, at a distance this painting acquires a vivacity of movement, which is its chief characteristic. The subject was a favourite one in seventeenth–century painting, where it provided an excuse for contrasts of light and for dinamic effects in the composition.

45. GIOVAN FRANCESCO GUERRIERI (Fossombrone 1589 – Pesaro 1659), *Loth and his daugters* (canvas: 1,43 × 1,65). Painted in Rome, 1617–1618. Mentioned by Manilli in 1650 as a Work of Archita Ricci. There exists a replica of it in the Galleria Doria in Rome.

56. MICHELANGELO DA CARAVAGGIO (Michelangelo Merisi. Caravaggio, 1573–1610), *St. Jerome* (canvas: 1,12 × 1,57). Formerly assigned to Ribera (Venturi). Longhi and Aldo de Rinaldis confirmed the attribution to Caravaggio, which had been claimed by Modigliani, following the suggestion of Bellori. Though beautifully painted, in a fluid and translucent manner, it is not Caravaggio's usual technique; and the scheme of the composition might suggest some painter, perhaps not even Italian, influenced by this master.

267. MICHELANGELO DA CARAVAGGIO (Michelangelo Merisi. Caravaggio, 1573–1610), *St. John the Baptist in the Desert* (canvas: 1,50 × 1,22). Frequent retouching during the nineteenth century has hardened the painting and male it so unattractive that some, such as Schudt, have been induced to exclude it from the list of Caravaggio's undisputed works. It was mentioned by Scipione Francucci who, in 1613, wrote a poem commemorating Cardinal Borghese's collection.

406. GIOVAN BATTISTA BENCI (Rome, flourished around 1625), *The Return of the Prodigal Son* (canvas: 1,10 × 1,48). One of Guercino's favourite subjects, repeated by him several times with slight variations. This painting, which was formerly attributed to Valentini, was referred to Benci by Longhi, following an annotation by Manilli (1650). There is a copy, which is also antique, in the Sacristy of S. Pietro in Vincoli, in Rome.

43. ANTONIO CARRACCI (Bologna, 1583–1618), *The Burial of Christ* (canvas: 1,23 × 1,68). First assigned to Annibale Carracci then to Lanfranco (Tietze), and finally attributed to Antonio by Longhi, after a comparison with the Flood by this artist in the Louvre. He was the son of Agostino Carracci and the nephew of Annibale, and died young, but he has left the mark of his own decided individuality among the paintings of his family.

519. JOHANNES WILHELM BAUR (Strasbourg: heard of until 1636), *View of the Borghese Villa* (parchment: 0,30 × 0,45). Signed and dated: Jo. Wilhelm Baur. Fecit 1636. The Villa is represented as Vasanzio planned it, with ornamentations and niches on the

façade, and with the double staircase which was destroyed at the time of Asprucci's restoration during the eighteenth century.

70. GUERCINO (Giovan Francesco Barbieri. Cento, 1591-1666), *Samson Presenting the Honeycomb to his Parents for the Prolongation of their Lives* (canvas: 1,12 × 1,46). In 1650 this painting already belonged to the Borgheses. It can therefore not be identified with the one mentioned by Venturi as being sold in 1658 to Sig. Tartaleoni, and for whih the painter was paid 660 scudi. However its scheme is certainly that of Guercino, and it can be compared with No. 42 in this same room even if, pictorically, it is much weaker.

53. DOMENICHINO (Domenico Zampieri. Bologna, 1581-1641), *Diana Hunting* (canvas: 2,25 × 3,20). An extensive landscape, full of light and precise detail, carried out with an easy grace that pauses to count the leaves on the trees, and strikes the bird in mid flight as it is caught by the fatal arrows, forms the background of this famous picture. In it the figures are charmingly grouped, and kept from becoming trivial by a miraculous stroke of ability, in conformity with the ingenuous spirit. The picture was carried off by force from the artist's studio by Cardinal Borghese who wished to secure it for his Gallery, and is justly considered to be one of its most important pieces. There are twenty drawings for studies of the nymphs in the Royal Collection of Windsor.

350. CESARE FRACANZANO (Monopoli di Bari, 1612-1656), *The Martyrdom of St. Ignatius* (canvas: 0,99 × 1,21). Formerly attributed to Luca Giordano. Longhi suggested the names of Agostino Beltrano and Cesare Fracanzano, and this last assignation has met with the most success. Although rather external in the dramatic effort of the representation, it is nevertheless a good picture, and characteristic of South Italian art during the middle of the seventeenth century.

136. CARAVAGGIO (Michelangelo Merisi. Caravaggio, 1573-1610), *A Boy with a Basket of Fruit* (canvas: 0,70 × 0,67). In 1607 a group of pictures in the Cavalier d'Arpino's studio were sequestrated by Paul V's exchequer, and amongst them was " a painting of a boy carrying a basket of fruit ,, which Longhi identifies as this one and dates to 1589. The youthful figure, bathed in a pure light, is a forerunner of the Magdalene and the Rest During the Flight into Egypt in the Doria Gallery, whereas the basket of fruit finds its immediate counterpart in the " Cestello ,, of the Ambrosiana in Milan.

534. CARAVAGGIO (Michelangelo Merisi. Caravaggio, 1573-1610), *A Young Ailing Bacchus* (canvas: 0,67 × 0,53). Also this picture, which was known as the Carracci Hunchback, was assigned to Caravaggio by Roberto Longhi. The leaden

41

colouring of the figure decided its attribution, and it is supposed to represent Caravaggio himself suffering from malaria. The fruit recalls the aforegoing picture.

455. CARAVAGGIO (Michelangelo Merisi. Caravaggio, 1573–1610), *David with the Head of Goliath* (canvas: 1,25 × 1,01). Bellori has minutely described this painting, and identified the head of Goliath as a self-portrait of the artist. It is an intermediary work between the Boy with the Basket of Fruit and the Madonna of the Palafrenieri, and shows Caravaggio's Lombard training, and his connections, in the colouring and still more in the lighting, with Savoldo's school of painting.

41. LIONELLO SPADA (Bologna, 1576–1522), *A Concert* (canvas: 1,80 × 1,42). Spada's loyalty to Caravaggio, whom he followed in all his adventures and wanderings, is also reflected in his painting; but this artist lacks the feeling for balance and harmony which makes the master great. In this composition the figures are too crowded, and the effect of light is lost in the projection of the surfaces.

110. CARAVAGGIO (Michelangelo Merisi. Caravaggio, 1573–1610), *The Madonna of the Palafrenieri* (canvas: 2,90 × 2,11). This canvas, which was painted in 1605 for the Confraternity of the Palafrenieri who intended it for an altar in St. Peter's, was refused by the Canons of the Basilica who thought the Blessed Virgin, St. Ann and the Infant Jesus were represented with too crude a realism. So it was bought by Cardinal Borghese and given a place of honour in his collection. It is one of the most powerful examples of Caravaggio's lighting effects, and marks the successful realization of his experiments in form. The composition is imposing and, in the very boldness of its invention, actually acquires, in its profound study of humanity, that divine essence which his conteporaries failed to recognize.

42. GUERCINO (Giovan Francesco Barbieri. Cento, 1591–1666), *The Return of the Prodigal Son* (canvas: 1,25 × 1,63). Bought in 1818 from the Lancellotti family, to whom it belonged. It is remarkable for its intense colouring, its scenic construction and its balance of form, and must therefore have been executed later than 1624, after Guercino returned from his second visit to Rome.

The sculpture:

CXVIII. GIAN LORENZO BERNINI (Naples, 1598–1680). *Jupiter and a Small Faun Taking Milk from the Goat Amalthea*, Longhi, following an indication by Sandrart, identified this as being Bernini's first work, carried out about 1615. It is obviously inspired from a Hellenistic motive. The legend of how the infant Jupiter was left on Mount Ida in order to escape the wrath of Saturn, is one of the favourite themes of that school of art, and was often repeated in the seventeenth century.

CCLXV. GIAN LORENZO BERNINI (Naples, 1598–1680). *Bust of Cardinal Scipione Borghese.*

CCLVI. GIAN LORENZO BERNINI (Naples, 1598–1680), *Bust of Cardinal Scipione Borghese.* Bernini did this bust in about 1625, but a vein in the marble came out in the chiselling, which cut across the Cardinal's forehead, and obliged him to do the whole thing over again. The replica does not possess the spontaneity of the first bust. Both were bought by the State in 1891 and, though cited in all the old guides, were not added to the collection until 1908.

CCXLIII. GIAN LORENZO BERNINI (Naples, 1598–1680), *A small bust of Paul V.* This precious little bust is mentioned by Rosini as standing on the table in Cardinal Scipione's private study. According to Fraschetti it was carried out between 1612 and 1622.

CCLXIX. GIAN LORENZO BERNINI (Naples, 1598–1680), *Model for the equestrian monument of Louis XIV of France* (terracotta). Given by Count Alessandro Contini Bonacossi in 1930. This is the model, carried out about 1678, for a monument to Louis XIV which Bernini was to have erected in the gardens of Versailles. The failures of Bernini's trip to France are well known. The monument was executed without taking the model into account, by the sculptor Girardon, but the model that has survived reveals an already worn out Bernini, preoccupied with the conventionalism of French art.

CLC. ALESSANDRO ALGARDI (Bologna, 1602–1654), *Sleep (a slumbering Cupid).* This sleeping boy crowned with poppy heads and with a dormouse fast asleep by his side, sculptured in touchstone, is mentioned by Passeri in the Borghese collection, as being by Algardi. The attribution passed through various doubtful moments, and was even completely disregarded, but no other name was ever assigned to the statue which, for that matter, can easily be included among the works of Bernini's great rival.

CVIIIC. *The genius of Sleeping Hercules.* Hellenistic style.

CCLI. *A fragmentary statue of a stag.* Roman period.

CCXLV. *An amazon and two warriors.* A much restored and reconstructed copy of an original by the Pergamene school.

ROOM XV

On the ceiling, between decorative motives by GIOVAN BATTISTA MARCHETTI, GAETANO LAPIS (Cagli, 1706–1758), painted an allegory of Aurora.

CCLX. *Head of a small child,* belonging to the Hellenistic period.

509. A FOLLOWER OF RUBENS (second half of the seventeenth century), *The Adoration of the Magi* (marble: 0,43 × 0,37). The derivation from Rubens is seen both in the composition and colouring, but this is so slightly marked that the picture can only be attributed to a follower. The artist has used the grey–veined marble in its natural state to form the background of the sky.

68. FEDERICO BAROCCI (Federico Fiori. Urbino, 1528–1612), *Aeneas Fleeing from the Fire of Troy* (canvas: 1,84 × 2,58). Signed and dated: Fed. Bar. Urb. Fac. MDXCVIII. Barocci painted this picture for Cardinal della Rovere, and it met with such success that he was obliged to make several copies of it, one of which was for the Emperor Rudolf II. It is full of melodramatic emphasis, and not one of the best by this Urbino artist, but the distant view is treated with great ability and the whole picture clearly expresses the painter's personalitv and artistic trend.

581. FEDERICO BAROCCI (Federico Fiori. Urbino, 1528–1612), *St. Michaelina*. A watercolour drawing for the picture of St. Michaelina in the Vatican Picture Gallery. There are other rough drawings for this painting in the Uffizi Gallery, However, in spite of variations in the background, this one seems more like the final sketch. It was published by Luigi Serra, and given to the Gallery in 1948 by General Teodorico Serra.

391. CAVALIER D'ARPINO (Giuseppe Cesari. Arpino, 1568–1640), *The Battle between Tullus Hostilius and the People of Veii* (canvas: 0,67 × 0,94). Rather than a first sketch, as Venturi thinks, for the large fresco in the Palace of the Conservators on the Capitol, this is more likely to be a copy carried out by the artist himself, perhaps for some admirer of the original work.

411. PETER PAUL RUBENS (Siegen, 1577–1640), *Mourning over the Body of Christ* (canvas: 1,80 × 1,37). Formerly attributed to Anthony van Dyk, and restored by Holdenburg to the youthful Rubens who must have painted it around 1605, during his second stay in Rome. It is a most effective picture owing to the warm light in the background, the expressive, though somewhat trivial, figure of the Magdalene, the double emphasis given to the grief of Nicodemus and Joseph of Arimathaea, and the pathetic upward gaze of the pious woman. But the potential quality of truly great art is revealed by the warm intonation of the painting and the perfect pattern to which the whole composition conforms.

278. JOHN BREUGHEL (a sixteenth–century follower), *Orpheus* (wood: 0,55 × 0,69). There are other copies of this picture; the best one is in the Prado Museum of Madrid, and another exists in the Sarasota Museum (Florida).

545. GIAN LORENZO BERNINI (Naples, 1598–1680), *Second Self–Portrait* (canvas: 0,56×0,44). Given by Baron Messinger in 1911. Luigi Grassi thinks it was painted after 1635. It is carried out in a different manner from the first portrait, and it certainly has the look of a self–portrait. It was attributed to Velasquez with whose painting it has obvious connections.

554. GIAN LORENZO BERNINI (Naples, 1598–1680), *A Youthful Self–Portrait* (canvas: 0,39 × 0,31). Bought in 1918 by Corrado Ricci and apparently painted around 1623. The fluid brushwork and transparent shadows, the keen, restless expression, and the novelty of the effect of light filtering through the chromatic impastation, make this pictorial testimonial worthy of being compared with Bernini's best marble achievements.

555. GIAN LORENZO BERNINI (Naples, 1598–1680), *Portrait of a Boy* (canvas: 0,36 × 0,30). This picture was added to the Borghese Gallery in 1919, and came from the Chigi collection. A comparison with the youthful self–portrait reveals the same hand in the technique, and in the use of colour and light. It is thought to be a portrait of Gian Lorenzo's brother, who was twelve years old when it is presumed this small canvas must have been painted.

353. SALVATOR ROSA (Arenella di Napoli, 1615–1673), *A Battle–scene* (canvas: 0,73 × 1,37). Remarkable for its decorative sense, and carried out with decided pictorial ability.

403. FEDERICO BAROCCI (Federico Fiori. Urbino, 1528–1612), *St. Jerome* (canvas: 0,97 × 0,67). Signed: Fred. Barocium Urb. Ping. In this painting Barocci's pictorial effort, always in search of effects, acquires a greater sense of proportion and a feeling for harmony which imposes itself upon his natural virtuosity.

376. ANDREA SACCHI (Rome, 1599–1661), *Portrait of Monsignor Clemente Merlini* (canvas: 1,50 × 1,37). In this portrait of the Auditor of the Sacred Rota, Bernini's great rival has achieved a superb personification both of the individual and of his time. Sacchi's colouring tends towards the luminosity of Venetian painting, which he acquired from the Bolognese school of the Carracci.

344. GASPARE CELIO (Roma, 1571–1640), *A Battle–scene* (wood: 0,56 × 1,40). Longhi proposes dating this picture between 1610 and 1612 when Celio was knighted. In fact he signs himself, at the bottom, on the right: " Gasparo Celio del Habito di Cristo f. ,,. It is one of the rare works of this painter who, though not one of the greatest, has managed to keep his own individuality among the manneristic followers of the Cavalier d'Arpino.

In the little corridor that leads to the next rooms, is a late Renaissance copy of the so-called " Cavaspina ,, , the bronze original of which is in the Museum of the Conservators on the Capitol.

298. RAFFAELLINO DA REGGIO (Raffaello Motta. Reggio Emilia, 1550–1578), *Tobias and the Angel* (wood: 1,07 × 0,69). Rather an exceptional picture by this Emilian artist who worked together with Lelio Orsi da Novellara, owing to the scarcity of his production. He also came to Rome, where he painted with the Zuccari brothers, whom he followed to Caprarola. There is a drawing for this picture in the Uffizi.

ROOM XVI

This ceiling, like those of the following rooms, is decorated by MARCHETTI, who has painted a representation of *Flora* in the centre. The white marble fireplace is lined with majolica tiles with the dragon and eagle, and has mythological subjects in bronze on the front. It belongs to the end of the seventeenth century.

Over the entrance door:

174. JACOPO PALMA THE YOUNGER (Venice, 1544–1628), *The Fall of Lucifer* (canvas: 0,68 × 1,46). A first sketch for a picture which was perhaps to have been larger but which has not survived. This last member of the great family of Venetian painters still maintains a strong feeling for colour.

26. JACOPO BASSANO (Jacopo da Ponte. Bassano, 1516–1592), *The Nativity* (canvas: 0,76 × 0,94). Here is a domestic scene where shepherds and animals mingle with singular intimacy. The rapid, creative touches of colour, and the sky streaked with light make this master a forerunner of the whole Venetian school, from Titian to Schiavone. The picture was mentioned by Manilli (1650) and assigned to Bassano by Roberto Longhi.

30. GIROLAMO SAVOLDO (Brescia 1480 c. – 1548), *Venus Asleep* (canvas: 1,30 × 2,12). Formerly attributed to Girolamo da Treviso by Coletti, who deciphered the painter's monogram on the tiny scroll in the bottom left–hand corner, and compared this canvas with the Nude in Vienna by Girolamo da Treviso. It is obviously derived from Giorgione's Venus and shows the various influences of his school which reached this painter through

the engravings of the Emilian masters. The fine landscape bathed in the warm light of the declining day, provides a soft accompaniment for the figure sleeping in the foreground. Datable to about 1510.

127. LEANDRO BASSANO (Leandro da Ponte. Bassano, 1557–1622), *The Holy Trinity* (copper: 0,52 × 0,43). Signed: Leand. Bassanus F. The painter has copied, with a certain freedom of detail, a large altarpiece in the church of Angarano, where Jacopo Bassano represented the Holy Trinity, which he in his turn took from Pordenone. Here, however, the landscape is different, the composition is more regular, and even the colouring is more subdued than in his father's altarpiece.

120. JACOPO BASSANO (Jacopo da Ponte. Bassano, 1516–1592), *A Sheep with its Lamb* (canvas: 0,30×0,51). In the ancient inventories of the Gallery, it bears the name of Titian. It is however without doubt a fragment of one of those vast pastoral scenes peculiar to the art of Bassano, and, in spite of evident disfigurements, the delicate quality of the composition warrants its assignment to Jacopo the Elder.

144. JACOPO BASSANO (Jacopo da Ponte. Bassano, 1516–1592), *The Last Supper* (canvas: 1,68 × 2,20). Longhi considers it to be Jacopo Bassano's masterpiece. It has a solemn grandeur of composition and the strong colouring is vital, as in this master's best work.

565. JACOPO BASSANO (Jacopo da Ponte. Bassano, 1516–1592), *The Adoration of the Magi* (canvas: 0,58 × 0,49). Formerly attributed to El Greco, for whose work that of Jacopo was often mistaken, and restored to its rightful author by Longhi. In his monograph on the Bassano family, Wart Arslan judges it to be by the school of Jacopo. However the exquisite blending of the colours, even though apparently clashing, confirms Longhi's attribution.

234. JACOPO BASSANO deriving from *The Adoration of the Magi* (wood: 0,50×0,41).

ROOM XVII

The canvas set in the centre of the ceiling is by GIUSEPPE CADES (Rome, 1750–1799). It relates the story of Walter, Duke of Angers, who, after many years of exile, returned as a beggar to the house of his daughter who no longer recognized him.

142. DOSSO DOSSI (Giovanni Luteri. Ferrara, 1489 ca.–1542), *St. Catherine of Alexandria* (canvas: 0,70 × 0,70). This

47

picture, which was mentioned by Manilli (1650) and confirmed by Roberto Longhi, belongs to Dosso's early maturity, and its link with the Ferrarese school of painting of that period is clearly marked. A useful comparison, in this respect, can be made with No. 240 in this room by Garofalo.

451. MAZZOLINO (Ludovico Mazzoli. Ferrara, 1478 ca.-1528), *The Adulteress* (wood: 0,29 × 0,17).

247. MAZZOLINO (Ludovico Mazzoli. Ferrara, 1478 ca.-1528), *The Nativity* (wood: 0,40 × 0,51).

223. MAZZOLINO (Ludovico Mazzoli. Ferrara, 1478 ca.-1528), *Doubting Thomas* (wood: 0,22 × 0,33). These three little pictures, together with No. 218 in the same room, form a pleasing testimonial of this artist's characteristics, which tend towards anecdotal and detailed narrative. The landscape, the figures, the whole representation, is imbued with a fabulous atmosphere, which finds its counterpart in Flemish painting, and to which the light sprinkling of gold adds a final legendary touch.

240. GAROFALO (Benvenuto Tisi. Ferrara, 1481–1559), *Madonna and Child with two Saints* (canvas: 0,74 × 0,84). The derivation of Garofalo's art is clearly shown in this picture, where he combines Dosso Dossi's precepts with the widely diffused influence of Raphael's art.

212. SCARSELLINO (Ippolito Scarsella. Ferrara, 1551–1620), *Venus and Adonis* (canvas: 0,95 × 1,20). Manilli mentions this picture among the first to be collected by Cardinal Scipione Borghese. Venus hastens to the dying Adonis, in a singularly broad landscape. The sky, streaked with horizontal light, is also vast, and the trees are few and the leaves light. The colouring, which keeps to a pleasing harmony of luminous pinks and yellows, gives the whole picture a festive atmosphere.

57. FRANCESCO FRANCIA (Francesco Raibolini. Bologna, 1450–1517), *St. Francis* (wood: 0,55 × 0,45). This picture was correctly assigned to Francesco Francia by Berenson, after Venturi's attribution to Marco Meloni had been discarded, and it was seen by the stigmata to represent St. Francis and not St. Anthony. Although it does not reach the clear height of his St. Stephan (No. 65) or the excellence of his St. George Killing the Dragon in the National Gallery of Ancient Art, it is still in keeping with the normal production of this Bolognese master, whose outlook is always dignified and honest.

390. ORTOLANO (Giovanni Benvenuti. Ferrara, born about 1485), *Christ Taken from the Cross* (wood: 2,64 × 2,02). This large panel painted for the church of S. Cristoforo degli Esposti in Ferrara, establishes this artist's personality which was for a long time confused with that of Garofalo, but which has quite a different potentiality. Aldo de Rinaldis points out how the

tall, well built figures might well be reproductions of wooden statuary groups. The landscape in the background is one of the most beautiful pieces of painting of this period of art.

226. SCARSELLINO (Ippolito Scarsella. Ferrara, 1551–1620), *Christ with his Disciples on the Road to Emmaus* (canvas: 0,86 × × 1,23). The strong light and the flashing colours of this painting connect it with the picture of Venus and Adonis (No. 212). Scarsellino's able use of colour is remarkable in both.

65. FRANCESCO FRANCIA (Francesco Raibolini. Bologna, 1450–1517), *St. Stephen* (wood: 0,75 × 0,53). " Vincentii Desiderii votum — Francie expressum manu „ is written on the piece of paper lying on the ground. This belongs to Francia's youthful period, and is a delicate piece of work, carried out with expert skill, in brilliant colours, and with such careful attention to detail that it resembles a large illuminated page. It also expresses a candour, and a pure open simplicity that reveal the very soul of the artist and the profound sincerity of his approach to art.

61. FRANCESCO FRANCIA (Francesco Raibolini. Bologna, 1450–1517), *Madonna and Child* (wood: 0,87 × 0,64). Ordered by Sister Dorotea Fantuzzi, of the Convent of St. Mary Magdalene in Bologna, as can be seen by an ancient inscription on the back of the panel. The rather cold composition shows the influence of the academic school, but it is accompanied by an extreme simplicity, which always comes out in Francia's work. This panel was often imitated by his followers, and especially by Boteri.

214. SCARSELLINO (Ippolito Scarsella. Ferrara, 1551–1620), *Diana and Endymion* (wood: 0,39 × 0,56). A small unpretentious composition, where the ancient myth is represented with decorative elegance.

169. SCARSELLINO (Ippolito Scarsella. Ferrara, 1551–1620), *Jesus in the House of the Pharisee* (wood: 0,39 × 1,20). This panel shows the decided influence of Venetian painting on Scarsellino, and especially that of the Bassanos whose pictures he copied and imitated, so that his work was often exchanged for theirs.

219. SCARSELLINO (Ippolito Scarsella. Ferrara, 1551–1620), *Venus at her Bath with Cupids* (canvas: 0,56 × 0,45). Here the artist's sole purpose is to compose a decorative motive, in which the figures are merely incidental.

224. GAROFALO (Benvenuto Tisi. Ferrara, 1481–1559), *The Nativity* (wood: 0,47 × 0,31). Like the Cavalier d'Arpino, this painter succeeds in acquiring a transparent grace in his smaller compositions, which is altogether charming.

218. MAZZOLINO (Ludovico Mazzoli. Ferrara, 1478–1528), *The Adoration of the Magi* (wood: 0,39 × 0,30). Mazzolino's

fresh narrative vein, in the Flemish style (as for example in the balcony) gives this little panel a festive air.

213. GAROFALO (Benvenuto Tisi. Ferrara, 1480–1559), *Madonna and Child with Saints* (wood: 0,39 × 0,30). A delicate composition carried out with a light hand in the style of the Ferrarese school.

222. SCARSELLINO (Ippolito Scarsella. Ferrara, 1551–1620), *Madonna and Child with St. John* (wood: 0,37 × 0,31). The inspiration of this family scene seems, as Venturi points out, to be taken from life. The burning of stubble, characteristic of the Po Valley, fills the landscape with distant lights.

Room XVIII

BÉNIGNE GAGNERAUX (Dijon, 1756–1795) painted the myth of Jupiter and Antiope on the ceiling.

277. PETER PAUL RUBENS (Siegen, 1577–1640), *Susanna and the Elders* (canvas: 0,94 × 0,67). Longhi considered it to be an autograph painting by Rubens, and van Puyvelde dated it to the artist's first visit to Rome. It reveals the chromatic excellence of this Flemish master, and his achievement of powerful expression by means of colour.

268. ANTHONY VAN DICK (a seventeenth-century Flemish follower), *Christ Crucified* (canvas: 0,86 × 0,58). This is a replica, or rather a copy, of the Crucifixion of Villa Albani, painted by van Dyck about 1628. Bellori mentions a third Christ on the Cross painted by this artist in Rome for Cardinal Bellarmino, but it can hardly be indentified with this one.

250. GERMAN SCHOOL OF THE SIXTEENTH CENTURY, *Portrait of Ludwig of Bavaria* (wood: 0,45 × 0,33). The figure is identified by the inscription: DEI GRACIA. LUDUVICUS. UTRIUSQUE BAVARIAE DUX. AETATIS. SUAE XXXVII.

274. MARTEN MANDEKENS (Antwerp, active around 1638, died in 1649–50), *The Visit of the Blessed Virgin to St. Elizabeth* (canvas: 1,01 × 0,77). Bought in 1819 by Prince Camillo Borghese as a painting by Rubens, and thought to be a first impression for the right wing of his Deposition in the Cathedral of Antwerp. A recent restoration brought out the signature and date: M. MANDEKENS ANTWERPIAE INVENIT C. FECIT 1630. This follower of Rubens must have taken the inspiration for his composition from an engraving, seeing that it is inverted. Neverthless the brilliant colouring and the play of low clouds show a distinct and well defined individuality.

269. PETER DE HOOCH (Utrecht, 1630–1677), *A Gathering round a Flute-player* (wood: 0,60 × 0,75). Peter, the son of

Charles de Hooch, followed Rembrandt, from whom he derived his calm luminous interiors. This panel was formerly attributed to Jean Leduc, then to van der Meer of Delft, but in 1839 Adolfo Venturi suggested the name of Peter de Hooch.

279. ABRAHAM CUYLEMBORCH (Utrecht, heard of between 1639 and 1658), *Diana at her Bath* (wood: 0,59 × 0,72). Signed and dated: A. CUYLEMBORCH F. 1666. This picture is chiefly remarkable for the fine treatment of the colouring and for the landscape bathed in golden light, which is carried out with rare feeling.

354. PAUL BRIL (Antwerp, 1554–1626), *View of a Port* (canvas: 1,12 × 1,56). This view, mentioned by Manilli (1650) must have been painted in Rome, for the Borgheses, between 1605 and 1626; that is to say between the election of Paul V and the painter's death, because the pontifical coat of arms of the Borghese pope can be seen on one of the yards. The view is expansive, and the picture is one on the most successful by this Flemish master, who has left so many examples of his ability as a landscape painter in the Borghese Gallery.

258–263. PAUL BRIL (Antwerp, 1554–1626), *Two Landscapes* (copper: 0,45 × 0,35).

241. LAMBERT ZUSTRIS (Amsterdam, second half of the sixteenth century), *A Birth* (canvas: 0,78 × 1,01). Formerly attributed to Bertoja, but identified by Peltzer as being a traditional picture by Lambert Zustris taken from a painting by his father Frederick, whose style was a combination of Flemish and Venetian influences. There are several versions of this composition, which must have conformed with the taste of the period.

291. DAVID TENIER THE YOUNGER (Antwerp, 1610–1690), *The Drinkers* (canvas: 0,78 × 0,99). The effect is pleasing, though it does not depart from the usual scene taken from everyday life.

272. PETER CODDE (Amsterdam, 1599–1678), *The Guardroom* (wood: 0,31 × 0,43). Signed: P. CODDE f. The monochrome intonation, in warm, golden shades of brown, is barely relieved by delicate touches of rose and blue in the soldiers uniforms, and especially in that of the Captain, which give the composition its tone. It is a fine piece of work by an aristocratic and rare artist.

273. GERRIT LUNDENS (Amsterdam, 1622–1683), *A surgical Operation* (wood: 0,31 × 0,35). Signed and dated: G. LUNDENS F. 1648.

253. FRANCK FRANCKEN (Antwerp: 1581–1642), *An Antiquary's Shop* (wood: 0,82 × 1,12). Signed: " Den. II Francis

Franck. P. inventor et fecit A. „. Paintings of interiors are quite common in Flemish art, and it is partly for this reason that they seldom depart from the representation of incidents, which are nothing more than pleasing scenes of everyday life.

284. AEGEUS VAN TILBORGH (Brussels, 1625–1678), *The Interior of an Inn* (canvas: 0,78 × 0,99). Though roughly treated it produces a decorative effect. On the barrel, to the right, is the signature: TILBORG.

ROOM XIX

The Scottish painter GAVIN HAMILTON (Lanark, 1723–1798), who helped to redecorate the Borghese Villa for Prince Marcantonio in 1794, frescoed *episodes from the life of Paris* on the ceiling of this room. Like in the other ceilings, he painted the *Death of Paris* in the centre; also the *Teaching given to Paris by Cupid*, the *Judgement of Paris*, and the *Meeting of Paris and Helena* in three of the medallions.

GIOVANNI PIANCASTELLI (Castelbolognese, 1845–1920), who was the first director of the Gallery after it passed to the State, radically restored the canvasses, which were in a damaged condition at the end of last century. The octagon representing *Archelaus delivering the young Paris to Hecuba* was done by VINCENZO CAMUCCINI (Rome, 1771–1844).

The four bas–reliefs over the doors, with figures of *Jupiter, Venus, Mars* and *Apollo* are by VINCENZO PACETTI (1746 ca.– 1820). They are of warm, amber–coloured Numidian marble, like the fireplace which is by the same artist.

In the centre of the room:

LVII. NICHOLAS CORDIER (1567–1612), *A girl with a dog and a small boy*. Enlivened by the use of different coloured marbles (antique grey, ravecciano, jasper, brocatel, onyx, alabaster, antique yellow and porphyry) in the elaborate chromatic style of the seventeenth century.

CCLXX. ALESSANDRO ALGARDI (Bologna, 1602–1654), *Bust of Cardinal Ginnasi*. A very fine bust from Palazzo Ginnasi, but found in the church of S. Maria della Vittoria by Cantalamessa who bought it for the Gallery in 1911. Cantalamessa published it as being the work of Bernini. Its attribution to Algardi, which was strongly advocated by Muñoz, was confirm ed by Aldo de Rinaldis who recognized its fine artistic quality.

CCLXVII. ALESSANDRO ALGARDI (Bologna, 1602–1654), *Bust of Vincenza Danesi*. Bought for the Borghese Gallery in 1907 by Ettore Modigliani who recognized it as a bust of

Vincenza Danesi taken from her tomb in S. Maria del Popolo. The identification of the sculptor, which passed from Bernini to Algardi, was however relegated to his school by de Rinaldis. Although it is not one of Algardi's highest achievements the style is obviously his, and there is no reason to deprive him of this realistic portrait.

85. PARMIGIANINO (Francesco Mazzola. Parma, 1503–1540), *Portrait of a Man* (wood: 0,52 × 0,42). In comparison with better known portraits by this painter, such as the so-called Antea in the National Museum of Naples, this one is extremely simple and might seem bare. However its psychological concentration is penetrating, and the projection of the figure in extremely elegant.

131. MARCO BASAITI (Venice, 1470; still active in 1530), *Eve* (wood: 1,50 × 0,82).

129. MARCO BASAITI (Venice, 1470; still active in 1530), *Adam* (wood: 1,50 × 0,82). Venturi supposes these two panels, like Dürer's Adam and Eve, formed the wings of a large altarpiece, and the long narrow proportions make this supposition feasible. The painting is rather coarse, and they certainly show Venetian characteristics. Probably the sheet of paper on the trunk of the tree, in the picture of Eve, bore a signature, but it is no longer legible.

217. DOSSO DOSSI (Giovanni Luteri. Ferrara, 1489–1542), *The Enchantress Circe* (canvas: 1,76 × 1,74). A scene of enchantment, perhaps generic, as Manilli says, who cited it in 1650 among the pictures of the Gallery. The sumptuously dressed figure of the Enchantress dominates the whole composition. Her gesture of lowering the torch to light it from the embers of the brasier is not one of action. It has an architectural function, and is for the purpose of forming a triangular scheme in the centre, round which the landscape falls naturally. Thus called into being as it were by magic, in a fabulous land full of luxurious vegetation and intoxicating colours, the Enchantress acquires an imposing dominion, and sums up all the splendour of the environment out of which the Orlando Furioso was taking shape.

184. BATTISTA DI DOSSO (Battista Luteri. Ferrara, died in 1548), *Psyche transported to Olympus* (wood: 0,92 × 0,75). Battista di Dosso executed the picture during his stay in Rome, repeating the motive of Raphael from the Farnesina superimposed on a Ferrarese landscape.

245. BATTISTA DI DOSSO (Battista Luteri. Ferrara, died in 1548), *Rest During the Flight into Egypt* (wood: 0,46 × 0,69). Although the painting of the two Luteri brothers is often so interchanged that it is difficult to decide how much is due to the one or the other, the freshness of this panel, its more

decorative style, and the less rigorous treatment of nature, favour its assignation to Battista di Dosso. It is a charming, daintily painted little picture.

150. FRANCESCO BASSANO (Francesco da Ponte. Bassano, 1549–1592), *The Adoration of the Magi* (canvas: 1,25 × 1,40). Francesco, the son of Jacopo, often painted pictures in collaboration with his father and in fact Longhi thinks both artists have had a part in the painting of this picture. Venturi and Aldo de Rinaldis attribute it to Francesco, whose characteristics are more in evidence.

86. PARMIGIANINO (?) (Francesco Mazzola. Parma, 1503–1540), *Portrait of a Boy* (canvas: 0,72 × 0,58). Formerly attributed to Raphael, but referred by Venturi and Longhi to Parmigianino whose elegant pose is certainly noticeable. It however reminded Aldo de Rinaldis more of Giuseppe Bedoli–Mazzola. On the folded envelope in the foreground is written: " In Roma ,,.

215. BATTISTA DI DOSSO (Battista Luteri. Ferrara, died in 1548), *The Nativity* (wood: 0,44 × 0,29). It looks as though it might be a first sketch for a larger painting that was perhaps never carried out and which, in any case, we know nothing about.

1. DOSSO DOSSI (Giovanni Luteri. Ferrara, 1489 ca.–1542), *Apollo and Daphne* (canvas: 1,19 × 1,16). Contemporary with the picture of the Enchantress Circe. The luxuriant, colourful landscape; the figure in the foreground (justifying its formerly having been called Orpheus, since the figure of Daphne passes almost unobserved); the fantastic colouring, its ingeniousness which breaks away from every traditional tie, proclaim the name of Dosso Dossi. It was listed in the 1833 inventory under the name of Michelangelo Caravaggio, but in the next one, dated 1854, it is already assigned to the Ferrarese school.

220. DOSSO DOSSI (Giovanni Luteri. Ferrara, 1489 ca.–1542), *The Adoration of the Shepherds* (wood: 0,35 × 0,28). Morelli thought this picture was also probably a first sketch for a larger altarpiece; his attribution to Dosso Dossi has been confirmed by later critics.

304. DOSSO DOSSI (Giovanni Luteri. Ferrara, 1489 ca.–1542), *Diana and Callisto* (canvas: 0,49 × 1,61). " Venus asleep with two wakeful nymphs by the Dossi ,, , as Manilli put it when describing the pictures of the Villa in 1650. It however represents the Nymph Callisto discovered, after her sin, by Diana who announces her future punishment. In this youthful picture, the yellow sunlight, the tender green of the vegetation, the white in the draperies, and even the landscape full of budding life, are witnesses of the initial stage of Dosso's art which was later so fully and magnificently expressed in his picture of Circe.

91. GIOVANNI ANTONIO PORDENONE (Pordenone, 1484–1539), *Judith* (canvas: 0,95 × 0,78). This attribution is due to Longhi who points out how the painting belongs " to that figurative art in which every action, even the most dramatic, is subject to the colour, where it expands and displays itself; and becomes an exuberant expression of life ,,.

225. DOSSO DOSSI (Giovanni Luteri. Ferrara, 1489 ca.–1542), *Gyges and Candaulus* (canvas: 0,41 × 0,55). King Candaulus, proud of his wife's beauty, summoned his slave Gyges to admire her. This little story, which has all the charm of an anecdote, was attributed to Scarsellino, but ought more correctly to be assigned to Dosso Dossi's youth. It must have been painted at about the same time as his Callisto and Diana (No. 304).

125. CORREGGIO (Antonio Allegri. Correggio, 1494–1534) *Danae* (canvas: 1,61 × 1,93). Vasari mentions this picture, which was painted, together with that of Leda and Io, for the coronation in Bologna of Charles V, to whom the Duke of Mantova intended to give it. It then travelled across Europe (from Prague to Stockholm, to Rome with Christina of Sweden, to London and to Paris) and was finally bought in 1824, for 285 English pounds, by Prince Borghese, who added it to the Collection. The story of how Jupiter transformed himself into a golden shower in order to penetrate more easily into the tower where Danae was confined, is told in low, harmonious tones. The figures and their surroundings are carried into an unreal atmosphere, and even the landscape seen throught the window is saturated with powdery light.

211. DOSSO DOSSI (Giovanni Luteri. Ferrara, 1489 ca.–1542), *Madonna and Child* (wood: 0,35 × 0,28). This picture also belongs to Dosso's early period, as shown by the vivacious play of light and colour which has a sparkling sheen, as well as by the gentle participation of the Madonna and Child in the representation.

ROOM XX

When painting the story of Psyche and Eros on the ceiling FRANCESCO NOVELLI (Venice, 1764–1836) took his inspiration from the Farnesina. In the centre *Psyche ascends to Olympus,* and in the surrounding partitions: *Venus complains of Eros to Jupiter; Jupiter sends Mercury in search of Eros; Eros appears before Jupiter; Venus is escorted by Mercury to the Meeting of the Gods.*

The fireplace, signed and dated by AGOSTINO PENNA (Rome, died in 1800), was carried it out in 1782. It is of white marble with two telamones in red porphyry on either side, and a sacrifical scene of the same marble sculptured on the front. Lined with majolica tiles.

In the centre of the room:

CCL. An idealized statue of a *young emperor*, in bronze, belonging to the Hellenistic period.

The doors, like those of the other rooms, were painted in the eighteenth century.

157. JACOPO PALMA THE ELDER (Serinalta, 1480–1528), *Holy Conversation, with St. Barbara and St. Justina, and two Devout Persons* (canvas: 1,35 × 1,94). After many changes of attribution, ranging from an anonymous painter of the Venetian school to Cariani, Lotto and Palma the Elder, this last has finally been chosen, owing to the solemnity of the representation, the clear, peaceful surroundings, and the smooth surfaces in the painting of the figures, preannouncing Palma's later work. The equilibrium and the sober colouring are particularly worthy of note.

130-132. GIORGIONE (Giorgio Barbarelli. Castelfranco Veneto 1478–1510), *Singer with flute – The Passionate Singer* (canvas: 1,05×0,77). The two singers, together with a third one which is no longer existing, were part of a big Concert, painted by Giorgione at the end of his life (1510), after the frescoes of the " Fondaco dei Tedeschi ,,. A recent restoring has enabled to reconstruct the composition of the figures, which have maintained a deep emotional strength. The red caps, the intense white, the gold of the mantle full of light, the shadow of the passionate melancholy, confirm a personnality without emphasis, the greatest among all Venetian painters of the sixteenth century.

147. TIZIANO VECELLIO (Pieve di Cadore, 1477–1576), *Sacred and Profane Love* (canvas: 1,18 × 2,79). There have been many interpretations given to this subject: Venus and Medea; Beauty adorned and Beauty unadorned; Heavenly and Earthly Love; Love and Chastity, besides the one which has met with most success: Sacred and Profane Love. It is certainly an allegory that has something to do with Spring, as shown by the details of the background; and it seems to have been taken from the Dream of Polyphylus by Francesco Colonna. Titian painted it somewhere around 1512, for the Aurelia family, whose coat of arms is on the front of the sarcophagus used as a basin; and it has the same resounding quality, as in the Flora of the Uffizi. The colouring is broadly laid on, and intensely luminous, and has a rare peacefulness. Equally full of peace and serene beauty are the tranquil waters of the landscape which is bathed in warm light and saturated with colour.

176. GIOVANNI BELLINI (Venice, died after 1516), *Madonna and Child* (wood: 0,50 × 0,41). Signed: Johannes Bellinus faciebat. Datable to between 1505 and 1510. It belongs to the master's mature period, when Giorgione and Titian had already paved the way for the mastery of colour in Venetian painting.

There is an affectionate atmosphere about the figures, and in the distant view which is extremely well intoned with the green curtain. The tree stands out charmingly in this lyrical landscape, the river runs peacefully and the mountains fade into the almost clowdless sky. The sense of drama is no longer present, as when the Blessed Virgin was in adoration of the Redeemer; there is no longer any feeling of separation. In this softened and more tender light the intercourse becomes human, and the Madonna is just a mother together with her child.

188. TIZIANO VECELLIO (Pieve di Cadore, 1477–1576), *St. Dominic* (canvas: 0,87 × 0,78). Signed: TICIANUS. Painted in a mature period, between the Sacred and Profane Love and Venus Blindfolding Cupid. The colour is finely laid on, the preparation rapid and barely covered. Here it is no longer a question of surfaces — which were a pretext for glorious expanses of colour — but the realization of character and individuality. The strongly characterized figure of St. Dominic is the expression of an idea.

396. ANTONELLO DA MESSINA (Messina, 1430–1479), *Portrait of a Man* (canvas: 0,30 × 0,24). Painted somewhere around 1473, before Antonello went to Venice, as shown by the chrystaline geometrization of the simple figure which has not yet been touched by the influence of Venetian painting. The vigorous, concentrated psychology is stupendous; and the expression of the eyes and the line of the lips, revealing astute satisfaction, are exceptionally vivid.

156. BONIFACIO VERONESE (Bonifacio Pitati. Verona, 1487–1553), *Christ in the House of the Zebedes* (canvas: 1,37 × 2,04). In spite of its being rather a poor picture, the architecture of the composition and the depth of colour bear witness of the vitality of Venetian painting.

450. VITTORE CARPACCIO (Venice, 1455–1526), *A Courtesan* (wood: 0,30 × 0,24). Carpaccio, who is a secondary artist but with quite a distinctive personality, has carried out this picture in an analytic manner, accentuating the ribbon plaited through the hair, the beads and the links of the necklace. The attribution is due to Cantalamessa who had the picture restored in 1916, with revealing results.

445. JACOPO PALMA THE ELDER (Serinalta, 1480–1528), *Portrait of a Man* (wood: 0,30 × 0,24). Dated: AN. AE. XXIII. 1510. This picture which was attributed to the school of Giovanni Bellini by Venturi, to Vittore Belliniano by Cavalcaselle, and to Mancini by Aldo de Rinaldis, conforms, as Longhi pointed out, with Palma the Elder's manner of painting. This can be immediately confirmed by a comparison with the figure of a devout person in picture No. 163 in the same room.

170. TIZIANO VECELLIO (Pieve di Cadore, 1477–1576), *Venus Blindfolding Cupid* (canvas: 1,18 × 1,85). Called the " Three Graces „ in the anciet inventories of the Gallery. However it represents Venus blindfolding Cupid, while the Nymphs come forward with his bow and arrow. Titian painted it when he was 88, and had completely changed his technique and outlook on art. The whole landscape is imbued with the blue and rose of the Dolomites, which is reflected in the sky; and the colour seems to fall in layers of light, anticipating the fantastic effect of the Impressionists.

137. PAOLO VERONESE (Paolo Caliari. Verona, 1528–1588), *The Preaching of St. John the Baptist* (canvas: 2,08 × 1,40). One of Paolo's early works, and mentioned in 1642 by Ridolfi as belong to the Ludovisi princes. Although unfinished, this canvas shows all the magnificence of Veronese painting: a feeling for decoration, fresh colours, elegant figures, and that particular way of bringing the story into the artists own times, as though it were a pleasant drawingroom piece with ladies and dandies clad in rich brocades and adorned with jewels. The fresh, gay tone of the colour is here reminiscent of the seventeenth century, and opens the way for the painting of the eighteenth century.

101. PAOLO VERONESE (Paolo Caliari. Verona, 1528–1588), *St. Anthony Preaching to the Fishes* (canvas: 1,12 × 1,57). Sent to Cardinal Scipione Borghese by the Patriarch of Aquileia, who wrote in 1607: " I am extremely glad you like the painting of Paolo Veronese „. It is later than the Preaching of the Baptist and can be dated to after 1560. The composition is free, as it always is with Paolo, and the colouring is also his — deeper, more sustained and vibrant, but still in his favourite shades of green, rose and blue. It tells the story of how, when St. Anthony came to preach in Rimini, all the inhabitants withdrew, so he turned to the fishes who hastened from every part of the sea to listen to him.

194. TIZIANO VECELLIO (Pieve di Cadore, 1477–1576), *The Scourging of Christ* (canvas: 0,86 × 0,58). This picture is also mentioned by Manilli (1650). Venturi is of the opinion that it was painted about 1560, and like the master's later pictures, it is carried out with impressionistic vigour on a coarse canvas, which contributes, with its heavy woof, to the effect of light in the painting. The able weilding of the technique is accompanied by a profound sense of suffering which, in the face of Christ, summarizes the suffering of the whole of humanity.

LIST OF ARTISTS AND THEIR WORKS

ILLUSTRATIONS

G. L. BERNINI: CARDINAL SCIPIONE BORGHESE, FOUNDER OF THE GALLERY

PALATII VILLAE BVRGHESIAE PROSPECTVS

G. G. BAUR: VIEW OF THE VILLA IN 1636

A. CANOVA: PAOLINA BORGHESE BONAPARTE

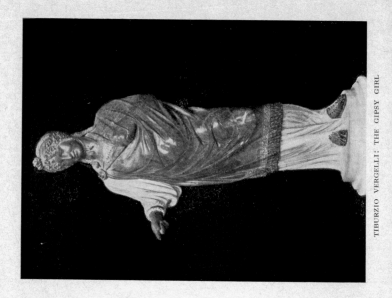

TIBURZIO VERGELLI: THE GIPSY GIRL

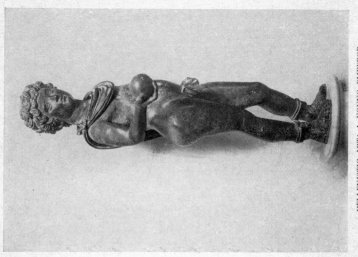

HELLENISTIC ART: A YOUNG EMPEROR

HELLENISTIC ART: THE RAPE OF CASSANDRA

HELLENISTIC ART: BACCHANALIA (FRAGMENT)

73

G. L. BERNINI: THE RAPE OF PROSERPINA

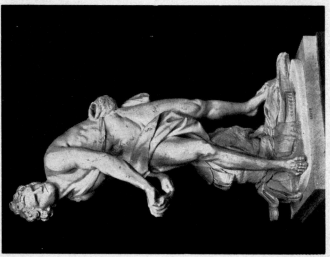

G. L. BERNINI: DAVID

74

G. L. BERNINI: APOLLO AND DAFNE

G. L. BERNINI: APOLLO AND DAPHNE (DETAIL)

G. L. BERNINI: APOLLO AND DAPHNE (DETAIL)

76

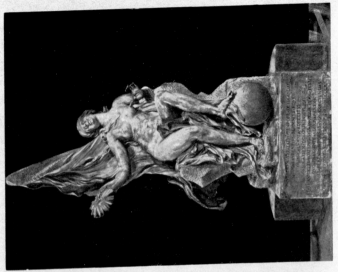

G. L. BERNINI: TRUTH

P. BERNINI: AENEAS AND ANCHISES

ROMAN ART
A BOY ASTRIDE A DOLPHIN

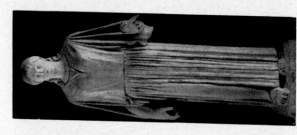

ARCHAIC GREEK ART
A FEMALE STATUE

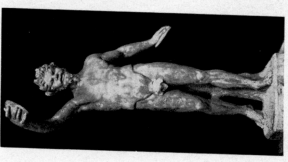

GREEK ART OF THE THIRD CENTURY
A DANCING FAUN (FROM A BRONZE
ORIGINAL)

LORENZO DI CREDI: MADONNA

SANDRO BOTTICELLI: MADONNA WITH ANGELS

PIERO DI COSIMO: ADORATION OF THE HOLY CHILD

FRA' BARTOLOMEO DELLA PORTA: HOLY FAMILY

PINTURICCHIO: CRUCIFIX AND SAINTS

RAFFAELLO: PORTRAIT

RAFFAELLO: PORTRAIT

82

RAFFAELLO: THE DEPOSITION

D. PULIGO: MARY MAGDALENE

MARIOTTO ALBERTINELLI: THE SAVIOUR

A. DEL SARTO: MADONNA

A. DEL SARTO: PIETÀ

BRONZINO: ST. JOHN THE BAPTIST

F. SALVIATI: PORTRAIT OF CARDINAL CERVINI

V. SALIMBENI: MADONNA

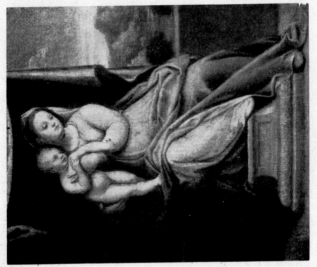

SANTI DI TITO: MADONNA

DOMENICHINO: DIANA HUNTING

ANN. CARRACCI: SAMSON

M. A. BASSETTI: CRIST TAKEN FROM THE CROSS

A. SACCHI: MONS. C. MERLINI

PIETRO DA CORTONA: MARCELLO SACCHETTI

90

G. L. BERNINI: PORTRAIT

G. L. BERNINI: SELF−PORTRAIT

ANN. CARRACCI:
HEAD OF A LAUGHING YOUTH

L. FONTANA:
PORTRAIT

N. DELL'ABATE: PORTRAIT

L. CAMBIASO: VENUS

P. TIBALDI: ADORATION

F. BAROCCI: ST. JEROME

RIDOLFO DEL GHIRLANDAIO: PORTRAIT

A. BRESCIANINO: ST. CATHERINE

S. PULZONE:
HOLY FAMILY

LELIO ORSI: ST. CECILIA
AND ST. VALERIAN

G. L. BERNINI: EQUESTRIAN STATUE OF LOUIS XIV (MODEL)

G. L. BERNINI: JUPITER AND THE GOAT AMALTHEA

A. ALGARDI: SLEEP

CARAVAGGIO: DAVID

CARAVAGGIO: ST. JOHN THE BAPTIST

CARAVAGGIO: THE MADONNA OF THE PALAFRENIERI

97

CARAVAGGIO: ST. JEROME

GUERCINO: THE PRODIGAL SON

ANTONIO CARRACCI: THE BURIAL OF CHRIST

A. TIARINI: RINALDO AND ARMIDA

G. HONTHORST: A CONCERT

99

SASSOFERRATO: MADONNA AND CHILD

DOMENICHINO: A SIBYL

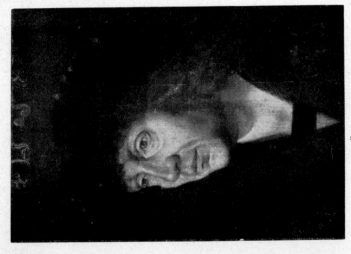

A. DÜRER: PORTRAIT

B. STRIEGEL: PORTRAIT DE CHARLES V

L. CRANACH: VENUS

P. P. RUBENS: THE DEPOSITION

P. P. RUBENS: SUSANNA AT HER BATH

F. BAROCCI: AENEAS FLEEING FROM THE FIRE OF TROY

DOSSO DOSSI: APOLLO

D. TENIERS: THE DRINKERS

DOSSO DOSSI: THE ENCHANTRESS CIRCE

DOSSO DOSSI: MADONNA AND CHILD

GAROFALO: MADONNA AND CHILD
WITH SAINTS

PARMIGIANINO: PORTRAIT

SCARSELLINO: HOLY FAMILY

L. MAZZOLINO: THE ADORATION OF THE MAGI

ORTOLANO: CHRIST TAKEN FROM THE CROSS

GAROFALO: HOLY CONVERSATION

SCARSELLINO: CHRIST IN THE HOUSE OF THE PHARISEES

DOSSO DOSSI: DIANA AND CALLISTO

L. ZUSTRIS: A BIRTH

F. FRANCIA: ST. STEPHEN

III

SODOMA: HOLY FAMILY   SODOMA: PIETÀ

M. D'OGGIONO: THE REDEEMER   GIAMPIETRINO: MADONNA

CORREGGIO: DANAE

P. VERONESE: ST. ANTHONY PREACHING TO THE FISHES

P. VERONESE: THE PREACHING OF ST. JOHN THE BAPTIST

J. BASSANO: A SHEEP WITH ITS LAMB

BASSANO: THE ADORATION OF THE SHEPHERDS

L. BASSANO: THE HOLY TRINITY

J. BASSANO: THE ADORATION OF THE MAGI

G. SAVOLDO: TOBIAS AND THE ANGEL

CARAVAGGIO: A BOY WITH BASKET OF FRUIT

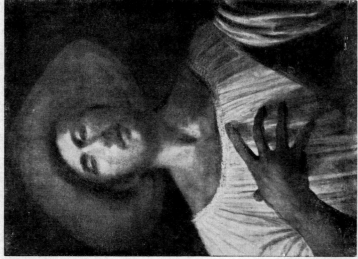

GIORGIONE (?): THE PASSIONATE SHEPHERD

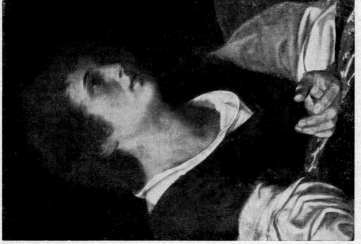

G. SAVOLDO: PORTRAIT

120

ANTONELLO DA MESSINA: PORTRAIT

BELLINI: MADONNA

V. CARPACCIO: A COURTESAN

J. PALMA IL VECCHIO: PORTRAIT

TIZIANO: SACRED AND PROFANE LOVE

TIZIANO: SACRED AND PROFANE LOVE (DETAIL)

TIZIANO: VENUS BLINDFOLDING CUPID

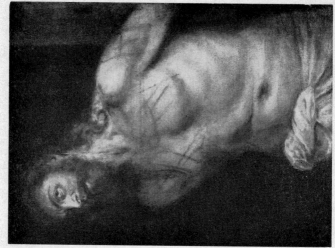

TIZIANO: ST. DOMINIC

TIZIANO: THE SCOURGING OF CHRIST

L. LOTTO: HOLY CONVERSATION

J. PALMA IL VECCHIO: HOLY CONVERSATION

PORDENONE: JUDITH

L. LOTTO: PORTRAIT

128

LIST OF ILLUSTRATIONS

129

LA
DIVINA COMMEDIA

Published by the Istituto Poligrafico dello Stato
to celebrate the 7th Centenary of the birth of
Dante Alighieri. Text and summaries edited
by Luigi Pietrobono. Miniatures selected
and annotated by Sergio Samek Ludovici.

DE–LUXE EDITION IN THREE VOLUMES. ONE
THOUSAND NUMBERED COPIES, LEATHER–BOUND
WITH CLOTH AND SILK CASE, PRINTED ON SPE-
CIAL WATERMARKED PAPER. 29 × 42 cm., 490 PAGES
OF TEXT AND 100 PLATES WITH 129 COLOUR
MINIATURES, REPRODUCED FROM CODICES GI-
RALDI, MARCIANO AND YATES THOMPSON (1965).

LIT. **250,000**

ISTITUTO POLIGRAFICO DELLO STATO
LIBRERIA DELLO STATO - Piazza G. Verdi, 10 - ROMA

IL DUOMO DI ORVIETO

BY ENZO CARLI

The six ample chapters of this volume expound the reasons why the CATHEDRAL OF ORVIETO transcends purely local interest and remains one of the loftiest and most perfect achievements of Italian civilization.

Although the reasons are not all to be found in the same historical period or cultural and stylistic tradition, they are interconnected not merely because they all refer to the same monument and are equally important and all the outcome of a religious tradition of art and iconography that is exceptional in its originality and loyalty to the motives which were its inspiration. It may well be that no other European Cathedral has the same recurrent spaciousness of expression.

The Author brings to the complex and often arduous problems which confront the scholar the benefits of his experience and sensitivity which often allow him to suggest original and enlightening solutions to many of them. They include various phases of the building of the Cathedral; the identification, or at least qualification according to style, of the great Masters who were responsible for the wonderful paintings and works of sculpture which adorn it and the masterpieces of goldsmithry and stained glass with which it is enriched. They range from Arnolfo di Cambio to Lorenzo Maitani, from Ugolino d'Ilario to Luca Signorelli and from Ugolino di Vieri to Giovanni di Bonino.

The illustrations in colour and black and white not only give an adequate idea of the richness and high artistic quality of the works studied in the text, but their range and accuracy make the volume an exceptionally attractive achievement in the field of publishing.

Summary: I – The Construction and Early Architects; II – The Reliefs on the Façade; III – Other external Sculptures; IV – The Earliest Paintings; V – The Frescoes in the " Cappella Nuova "; VI – The Reliquary and Stained Glass.

Description and price of the volume:

Size 23 × 25 cm., 148 pp. of text on hand–made paper, with two inserted collotype plates, 276 plates, 123 of them in colour. Bound in yellow cloth with pastel lettering, colour plastic dust–jacket. (Ed. 1965).

Lire **35,000**

ISTITUTO POLIGRAFICO DELLO STATO

LIBRERIA DELLO STATO - Piazza G. Verdi, 10 - ROMA

COLLANA DEGLI
ITINERARI DEI MUSEI, GALLERIE
E MONUMENTI D'ITALIA

(a cura del Ministero della Pubblica Istruzione – Direzione Generale
delle Antichità e Belle Arti)

Preceduti da un cenno storico di ciascuna raccolta d'arte, questi " ITINERARI „ (nel formato 12,5 × 18,5 in brossura), redatti da autori altamente qualificati, sono utilissimi per tutti i turisti che si accingono a visitare i Musei e Gallerie d'Italia.

AREZZO.

BERTI L. – IL MUSEO DI AREZZO.

(N. 103 della serie) testo italiano, 76 pp. con 62 ill. .... L. 650

ASSISI.

ZOCCA E. – ASSISI E DINTORNI.

(N. 81 della serie) testo italiano, 92 pp. con 59 ill. e 4 piante...... L. 500
Testo inglese .... » 800
Testo tedesco .... » 400
Testo francese .... » 800

BAGNAIA.

CANTONI A. – VILLA LANTE.

(N. 94 della serie) testo italiano, 56 pp. con 46 ill. e 2 piante...... L. 500
Testo francese .... » 450

BENEVENTO.

ROTILI M. – MUSEO DEL SANNIO DI BENEVENTO.

(N. 111 della serie) testo italiano, 48 pp. con 100 ill. ...... L. 1200

BOLZANO.

ARSLAN E. – IL MUSEO DELL'ALTO ADIGE A BOLZANO.

(N. 77 della serie) testo italiano, 74 pp. con 62 ill. .... L. 200

CAPRI.

MAIURI A. – STORIA E MONUMENTI.

(N. 93 della serie) testo italiano, 128 pp. con 65 ill. e 6 piante.. L. 600
Testo inglese .... » 700
Testo tedesco .... » 700
Testo francese .... » 700

CERVETERI.

PALLOTTINO M. – LA NECROPOLI DI CERVETERI.

(N. 70 della serie) testo italiano, 52 pp. con 34 ill. e 2 piante...... L. 600
Testo inglese .... » 600
Testo tedesco .... » 600

CIRCEO - TERRACINA - FONDI.

Aurigemma S., Bianchini A., De Santis A. – CIRCEO – TERRACINA – FONDI.

(N. 97 della serie) testo italiano, 112 pp. con 69 ill. .... L. **600**

Testo tedesco .... » **650**

Testo francese .... » **650**

ERACLEA MINOA.

De Miro E. – ANTIQUARIUM E LA ZONA ARCHEOLOGICA DI ERACLEA MINOA.

(N. 110 della serie) testo italiano, 52 pp. con 40 ill. .... L. **750**

ERCOLANO.

Maiuri A. – ERCOLANO.

(N. 53 della serie) testo italiano, 128 pp. con 81 ill. e 2 piante L. **800**

Testo inglese .... » **650**

Testo tedesco .... » **750**

Testo francese .... » **850**

ESTE.

Fogolari G. – IL MUSEO NAZIONALE ATESTINO IN ESTE.

(N. 59 della serie) testo italiano, 76 pp. con 78 ill. e 3 piante...... L. **700**

Testo tedesco .... » **800**

FAENZA.

Liverani G. – IL MUSEO DELLE CERAMICHE IN FAENZA.

(N. 57 della serie) testo italiano, 76 pp. con 103 ill. e 2 piante .... L. **350**

FERRARA.

Aurigemma S., Alfieri N. – IL MUSEO NAZIONALE DI SPINA.

(N. 95 della serie) testo italiano, 83 pp. con 47 ill. e 6 piante...... L. **500**

FIESOLE.

De Agostino A. – SCAVI E MUSEO DI FIESOLE.

(N. 83 della serie) testo italiano, 64 pp. con 54 ill................. L. **600**

Testo inglese .... » **750**

Testo tedesco .... » **750**

FIRENZE.

Pacchioni G. – LA GALLERIA DEGLI UFFIZI.

(N. 8 della serie) testo italiano, 148 pp. con 179 ill. e 4 piante .... L. **800**

Testo inglese .... » **900**

Testo tedesco .... » **550**

Rossi F. – IL MUSEO NAZIONALE DI FIRENZE (Palazzo del Bargello).

(N. 9 della serie) testo italiano, 104 pp. con 179 ill. e 3 piante .... L. **750**

Sinibaldi G. – IL PALAZZO VECCHIO DI FIRENZE.

(N. 39 della serie) testo italiano, 68 pp. con 78 ill. e 5 piante .. (*in ristampa*)

Testo inglese .... L. **300**

Testo tedesco .... » **300**

Testo francese .... » **300**

Chiarelli L. – LA GALLERIA PALATINA A FIRENZE.

(N. 41 della serie) testo italiano, 84 pp. con 135 ill. .... L. **350**

Testo inglese .... » **500**

Rusconi J. A. – IL MUSEO DEGLI ARGENTI IN FIRENZE.

(N. 42 della serie) testo italiano, 65 pp. con 97 ill. e 3 piante...... (*esaurito*)

Testo tedesco ed italiano L. **250**

Testo francese ed italiano » **250**

PROCACCI U. – LA GALLERIA DEL-
L'ACCADEMIA DI FIRENZE.

(N. 52 della serie) testo italiano, 100
pp. con 80 ill., 2 piante e un fascicoletto
di aggiornamenti .... L. **450**

Testo inglese .... (*esaurito*)

FORLI'.

ARFELLI A. – LA PINACOTECA E I
MUSEI COMUNALI DI FORLÌ.

(N. 47 della serie) testo italiano, 64 pp.
con 89 ill. e 3 piante...... L. **250**

GAETA, FORMIA E MINTURNO.

AURIGEMMA S., DE SANTIS A. – GAETA,
FORMIA E MINTURNO.

(N. 92 della serie) testo italiano, 104
pp. con 59 ill. .... L. **600**

GENOVA.

GROSSO O. – IL MUSEO CHIOSSONE
DI GENOVA.

(N. 31 della serie) testo italiano, 78 pp.
con 120 ill. e 2 piante .... L. **250**

L'AQUILA.

MATTHIAE G. – IL CASTELLO DEL-
L'AQUILA E IL MUSEO NAZIO-
NALE ABRUZZESE.

(N. 101 della serie) testo italiano, 60
pp. con 51 ill. .... L. **500**

LECCE.

BERNARDINI M. – MUSEO PROVIN-
CIALE DI LECCE.

(N. 99 della serie) testo italiano, 50 pp.
con 47 ill. e 2 piante...... L. **400**

MILANO.

TEA E. – LA PINACOTECA AMBRO-
SIANA DI MILANO.

(N. 15 della serie) testo italiano, 43 pp.
con 52 ill. e 2 piante .... (*esaurito*)

Testo tedesco ed italiano L. **250**

Testo francese ed italiano » **250**

MORASSI A. – IL MUSEO POLDI–PEZ-
ZOLI IN MILANO.

(N. 21 della serie) testo italiano, 60 pp.
con 77 ill. e 3 piante...... L. **700**

Testo tedesco ed italiano » **250**

MORASSI A. – IL PALAZZO REALE DI
MILANO.

(N. 55 della serie) testo italiano, 81 pp.
con 69 ill. e 2 piante...... L. **250**

MODENA.

QUINTAVALE A. – LA GALLERIA
ESTENSE DI MODENA.

(N. 25 della serie) testo italiano, 92 pp.
con 100 ill. .... L. **800**

Testo tedesco .... » **900**

NAPOLI.

QUINTAVALLE A. O. – LA PINACOTECA
DEL MUSEO NAZIONALE DI NA-
POLI.

(N. 12 della serie) testo italiano, 64 pp.
con 87 ill. e 3 piante...... (*esaurito*)

Testo inglese ed italiano (*esaurito*)

Testo tedesco ed italiano (*esaurito*)

Testo francese .... L. **200**

PESCE G. – IL MUSEO NAZIONALE DI
NAPOLI. (Oreficeria – Toreutica –
Gliptica – Vitriaria – Ceramica).

(N. 19 della serie) testo italiano, 75 pp.
con 41 ill. e 3 piante...... (*esaurito*)

Testo inglese ed italiano L. **250**

MAIURI A. – I CAMPIFLEGREI (DAL-
SEPOLCRO DI VIRGILIO ALL'AN-
TRO DI CUMA).

(N. 32 della serie) testo italiano, 168
pp. con 94 ill. e 1 cartina L. **700**

Testo inglese .... » **800**

Testo tedesco .... » **1000**

Testo francese .... » **800**

ROMANO T. E. – IL MUSEO «DUCA DI MARTINA» NELLA VILLA «LA FLORIDIANA» DI NAPOLI.

(N. 50 della serie) testo italiano, 102 pp. con 87 ill. e 3 cartine   L. 450

NEMI.

MORETTI G., CAPRINO C. – IL MUSEO DELLE NAVI ROMANE DI NEMI.

(N. 72 della serie) testo italiano, 58 pp. con 30 ill. .... L. 300

OSTIA.

CALZA G., BECATTI G. – OSTIA.

(N. 1 della serie) testo italiano, 116 pp. con 63 ill. e 4 piante...... L. 900

Testo inglese .... » 1000

Testo tedesco .... » 1000

Testo francese .... » 800

CALZA R. – MUSEO OSTIENSE.

(N. 79 della serie) testo italiano, 172 pp. con 60 ill. .... L. 1000

PAESTUM.

SESTIERI P. C. – PAESTUM: LA CITTÀ, LA NECROPOLI PREISTORICA.

(N. 84 della serie) testo italiano, 70 pp. con 35 ill. e 8 piante...... L. 700

Testo inglese .... » 750

Testo tedesco .... » 750

Testo francese .... » 750

SESTIERI P. C. – IL NUOVO MUSEO DI PAESTUM.

(N. 89 della serie) testo italiano, 30 pp. con 23 ill. e 2 piante...... L. 450

Testo inglese .... » 500

Testo tedesco .... » 500

PALERMO.

DELOGU R. – GALLERIA NAZIONALE DELLA SICILIA.

(N. 105 della serie) testo italiano, 136 pp. con 100 ill. e 2 piante   L. 800

MARCONI P. – IL MUSEO NAZIONALE DI PALERMO.

(N. 11 della serie) testo italiano
(in ristampa)

PALESTRINA.

IACOPI G. – IL SANTUARIO DELLA FORTUNA PRIMIGENIA E IL MUSEO ARCHEOLOGICO PRENE-STINO.

(N. 100 della serie) testo italiano, 68 pp. con 60 ill. .... L. 600

PARMA.

SORRENTINO A. – LA GALLERIA DI PARMA.

(N. 5 della serie) testo italiano, 63 pp. con 60 ill. e 3 piante...... (esaurito)

Testo tedesco ed italiano   L. 250

MONACO G. – IL MUSEO DI ANTI-CHITÀ DI PARMA.

(N. 74 della serie) testo italiano, 48 pp. con 38 ill. .... L. 200

PAVIA.

MORASSI A. – LA CERTOSA DI PAVIA.

(N. 65 della serie) testo italiano, 96 pp. con 102 ill. .... L. 600

PERUGIA.

CALZONI U. – IL MUSEO ARCHEO-LOGICO NAZIONALE DELL'UM-BRIA – SEZIONE PREISTORICA.

(N. 71 della serie) testo italiano, 74 pp. con 200 ill. .... (in ristampa)

SANTI F. – LA GALLERIA NAZIONA-LE DELL'UMBRIA (PINACOTECA) DI PERUGIA.

(N. 90 della serie) testo italiano, 74 pp. con 52 ill. .... L. 700

Testo inglese .... L. 800

Testo tedesco .... » 650

PIAZZA ARMERINA.

GENTILI G. V. – LA VILLA IMPERIA-
LE DI PIAZZA ARMERINA.

(N. 87 della serie) testo italiano, 92 pp.
con 41 ill. e 1 pianta...... L. **600**

Testo inglese .... » **700**

Testo tedesco .... » **700**

Testo francese .... » **700**

POMPEI.

MAIURI A. – POMPEI.

(N. 3 della serie) testo italiano, 180
pp. con 18 ill. nel testo, 113 f. t. e 2
piante .... L. **900**

Testo inglese .... » **900**

Testo tedesco .... » **1000**

Testo francese .... » **900**

Testo spagnolo ......(*in ristampa*)

POMPOSA.

SALMI M. – L'ABBAZIA DI POMPOSA.

(N. 62 della serie) testo italiano, 41 pp.
con 44 ill. e 2 piante...... L. **400**

Testo inglese .... » **500**

Testo tedesco .... » **250**

Testo francese .... » **500**

POPULONIA.

DE AGOSTINO A. – POPULONIA, LA
CITTÀ E LA NECROPOLI.

(N. 109 della serie) testo italiano, 56
pp. con 25 ill. .... L. **750**

POTENZA.

SESTIERI–BERTARELLI M. – MUSEO AR-
CHEOLOGICO.

(N. 96 della serie) testo italiano, 77 pp.
con 46 ill. e 3 piante...... L. **450**

RAVENNA.

ARFELLI A. – LA GALLERIA DELL'AC-
CADEMIA DI BELLE ARTI DI RA-
VENNA.

(N. 49 della serie) testo italiano, 50 pp.
con 68 ill. e 3 piante...... L. **200**

ROMA.

BUCARELLI P. – LA GALLERIA NAZIO-
NALE D'ARTE MODERNA IN RO-
MA.

(N. 13 della serie) testo italiano, 146
pp. con 183 ill. .... (*esaurito*)

Testo inglese .... L. **600**

Testo francese .... » **550**

RICCI C., COLINI A. M., MARIANI V. –
VIA DELL'IMPERO

(N. 24 della serie) testo italiano, 141
pp. con 147 ill. e una pianta (*esaurito*)

Testo tedesco .... L. **350**

Testo francese .... (*esaurito*)

ZERI F. – LA GALLERIA SPADA IN
ROMA.

(N. 27 della serie) testo italiano, 61 pp.
con 54 ill. e 2 piante...... L. **500**

Testo inglese .... » **700**

Testo tedesco .... » **700**

Testo francese .... » **700**

SERRA L. – IL MUSEO ARTISTICO
INDUSTRIALE DI ROMA.

(N. 33 della serie) testo italiano, 47 pp.
con 70 ill. e 2 piante...... L. **200**

STEFANI E. – IL MUSEO NAZIONALE
DI VILLA GIULIA.

(N. 38 della serie) testo italiano, 77 pp.
con 101 ill. e 3 piante .... (*esaurito*)

Testo inglese .... L. **350**

Sestieri P. C. – MUSEO DELLA PREI-
STORIA E PROTOSTORIA DEL
LAZIO.

(N. 58 della serie) testo italiano, 60 pp.
con 37 ill. .... L. **700**

Delle Pergola P. – LA GALLERIA
BORGHESE IN ROMA.

(N. 43 della serie) testo italiano, 130
pp. con 115 ill. e 2 piante   L. **800**

Testo inglese .... » **800**

Testo tedesco con 4 tavole
a colori .... » **800**

Testo francese .... » **800**

Testo spagnolo.......... » **800**

Della Pergola P. – VILLA BORGHESE.

(N. 106 della serie) testo italiano, 78
pp. con 64 ill. e 2 tavole   L. **1000**

Romanelli P. – IL FORO ROMANO.

(N. 44 della serie) testo italiano, 104
pp. con 72 ill. e 3 piante   L. **700**

Testo inglese .... » **800**

Testo tedesco .... » **800**

Testo francese .... » **800**

Romanelli P. – IL PALATINO.

(N. 45 della serie) testo italiano,
nuova ediz., 72 pp. con 62 ill. e 4
piante .... L. **500**

Testo inglese .... » **600**

Testo tedesco .... » **600**

Testo francese .... » **350**

Floriani Squarciapino M. – IL MUSEO
DELLA VIA OSTIENSE.

(N. 91 della serie) testo italiano, 62 pp.
con 26 ill. .... L. **300**

Moretti G. – ARA PACIS AUGUSTAE.

(N. 67 della serie) testo italiano, 45 pp.
con 27 ill. e 1 pianta...... L. **500**

Testo inglese .... » **600**

Testo tedesco .... » **600**

Golzio V. – LA GALLERIA E LE COL-
LEZIONI DELLA ACCADEMIA DI
SAN LUCA IN ROMA.

(N. 69 della serie) testo italiano, 72 pp.
con 85 ill. e 2 piante...... L. **700**

Aurigemma S. – LE TERME DI DIO-
CLEZIANO ED IL MUSEO NAZIO-
NALE ROMANO.

(N. 78 della serie) testo italiJno, 280
pp. con 148 ill. e 7 piante   L. **1200**

Testo inglese .... » **1300**

Testo tedesco .... » **1300**

Testo francese .... » **1200**

Aurigemma S. – LA BASILICA SOT-
TERRANEA NEOPITAGORICA DI
PORTA MAGGIORE IN ROMA.

(N. 104 della serie) testo italiano, 56
pp. con 42 ill. e grafici .. L. **500**

Marchetti–Longhi G. – L'AREA SA-
CRA DEL LARGO ARGENTINA.

(N. 102 della serie) testo italiano, 130
pp. con 107 ill. e 1 pianta   L. **700**

Lavagnino E. – CASTEL S. ANGELO –
MUSEO.

(N. 82 della serie) testo italiano, 80 pp.
con 68 ill. .... L. **300**

Testo inglese .... » **350**

Testo tedesco .... » **350**

Testo francese .... » **350**

Gerlini E. – LA VILLA DELLA FAR-
NESINA.

(N. 80 della serie) testo italiano, 77 pp.
con 48 ill. .... L. **300**

SORRENTO.

Morazzoni G. – IL MUSEO CORREA-
LE DI SORRENTO.

(N. 66 della serie) testo italiano, 54 pp.
con 74 ill. e 3 piante...... L. **200**

SPERLONGA.

IACOPI G. – L'ANTRO DI TIBERIO ED IL MUSEO ARCHEOLOGICO.

(N. 107 della serie) testo italiano, 32 pp. con 60 ill. e 2 piante   L. **800**

Testo inglese .... » **900**

Testo tedesco .... » **900**

TARANTO.

DRAGO C. – IL MUSEO NAZIONALE DI TARANTO.

(N. 20 della serie) testo italiano, 96 pp. con 114 ill. e 3 piante .... L. **500**

TIVOLI.

MANCINI G. – VILLA ADRIANA E VILLA D'ESTE.

(N. 34 della serie) testo italiano: aggiornata, 55 pp. con 62 ill. e 3 piante .... L. **700**

Testo inglese .... » **750**

Testo tedesco .... » **750**

TORINO.

CARDUCCI C. – IL MUSEO DI ANTICHITÀ DI TORINO (COLLEZIONI PREISTORICHE E GRECO–ROMANE).

(N. 6. della serie) testo italiano, 76 pp. con 79 ill. .... L. **650**

GABRIELLI N. – LA GALLERIA SABAUDA A TORINO.

(N. 16 della serie) testo italiano, 72 pp. con 90 ill. .... L. **700**

Testo francese .... L. **800**

GABRIELLI N. – LA GALLERIA DELL'ACCADEMIA ALBERTINA DI TORINO.

(N. 28 della serie) testo italiano, 43 pp. con 72 ill. e 2 piante...... L. **200**

TRAPANI.

BIAGI L. – IL MUSEO PEPOLI IN TRAPANI.

(N. 46 della serie) testo italiano, 54 pp. con 84 ill. e 3 piante...... L. **1000**

TUSCOLO.

BORDA M. – TUSCOLO.

(N. 98 della serie) testo italiano, 63 pp. con 40 ill. e a piante .... L. **500**

URBINO.

ZAMPETTI P. – IL PALAZZO DUCALE DI URBINO E LA GALLERIA NAZIONALE DELLE MARCHE.

(N. 86 della serie) testo italiano, 74 pp. con 55 ill. .... L. **500**

Testo tedesco .... » **350**

Testo francese .... » **450**

VALLOMBROSA.

KOVACEVICH C. – L'ABBAZIA DI VALLOMBROSA.

(N. 85 della serie) testo italiano, 44 pp. con 31 ill. e 2 piante...... L. **250**

VEIO.

DE AGOSTINO A. – VEIO: LA STORIA, I RUDERI, LE TERRECOTTE.

(N. 108 della serie) testo italiano, 84 pp. con 42 ill. .... L. **800**

VELLEIA.

AURIGEMMA S. – VELLEIA.

(N. 73 della serie) testo italiano, 88 pp. con 81 ill. .... L. **650**

INDIRIZZARE LE RICHIESTE A:

Istituto Poligrafico dello Stato
LIBRERIA DELLO STATO - PIAZZA VERDI, 10 - 00100 ROMA

UPPER FLOOR

PRICE LIT. 1000